DANCING ADDICTION

A mother's journey with her drug-addicted son

By:
Gee Abrahams and Lily Bright

DANCING ADDICTION
A Mother's Journey with her drug-addicted Son

Published by Light Reflectors Publishers

Cape Town, South Africa

lightreflectorspub@gmail.com

ISBN 978-0-7961-1191-3

eISBN 978-0-7961-1192-0

2 4 6 8 10 9 7 5 3

Layout and cover design by Boutique Books

Printed in South Africa by Bidvest Data

DANCING ADDICTION

This is a work of fiction based on real events

You will learn
by reading
but
you will understand
with love.

Shams of Tabriz

What had I done wrong?
Was I not attentive enough?
Why was this happening to me?
Who am I?
What am I?
What is my purpose?

Consumed by questions, guilt and self-doubt she knew she couldn't afford to lose hope.

This book is dedicated to my children
Mikhail and Sarah
and to those I met along the path of addiction

Contents

Introduction

I faced two main challenges when I confronted drug addiction in my son. These challenges were the accepted beliefs of society and that I was a woman.

I began to search far and wide for answers. At times, I looked in places I never knew existed before I started this journey. For example, I came across the German philosopher, Nietzsche. In the preface to *Beyond Good and Evil*, he summed the situation up perfectly.

"Supposing that Truth is a woman – what then? Is there not ground for suspecting that all philosophers, in so far as they have been dogmatists, have failed to understand women – that the terrible seriousness and clumsy importunity with which they have usually paid their addresses to truth, have been unskilled and unseemly methods for winning a woman?

Certainly, she has never allowed herself to be won; and at present, every kind of dogma stands with sad and discouraged men – If indeed it stands at all!"

Dogma! That is what I was up against, and worse I found all that dogma within myself. I knew I needed to break free from it, so I decided to write my story with my faithful, truthful friend, Lily.

As we wrote together, I realised that we were not only bound by European conventions and dogmatic beliefs.

I was determined to live life on my terms, without the constraints of society's expectations.

Writing my story with Lily was a cleansing experience. It allowed me to explore my deepest thoughts and emotions and challenged the dogmas that had held me back for so much of my life. Together, we broke down the walls of tradition and convention and discovered a new sense of freedom and creativity.

As I continued to write, I realised that my story was not just my own but that of all women who have struggled to break free from the constraints of society.

I was determined to live my life on my terms and to inspire others to do the same.

With Lily by my side, I felt empowered to speak my truth and embrace my unique voice. I knew there would be obstacles and challenges ahead, but I was ready to face them head-on.

And so, by now, we are very free spirits indeed. And me, being a woman and a mother too!

Warmly,
Ella Moon and Lily Bright
The Bay of Falsehood, 2018

Prologue

A Separate Introduction

The Pen and Sentence

As if in a coffin, my son, Luke Moon found himself in the holding cells of *Wasteland*[1] Prison. Allow me to share with you the details of the case that led him to this situation. It was a complex matter involving a challenging organisation and a time for healing.

Before I continue, I should clarify something: there is a grave misconception about the power of what a mother can do. The prisoners of the *Sun*[2] may not be aware of the light of the *Moon*[3], but as a woman I know full well of the power of the Moon and the love that she holds.

Back to the holding cell: it was a nightmare, with the stench of urine and dirt hanging in the air.

Luke couldn't wait to break free from the shackles he found himself in. But, despite his desire to escape, he remained confined behind those walls, with the door locked, for three unending days and even longer nights. He was suffering not only because of the conditions or the darkness, but also because he was going through withdrawal from the poison that had landed him here.

---

1 Wasteland refers to spiritual, intellectual and social decay, brokenness, degenerating society, barren and uncultivated land, etc.

2 The Sun is the symbolic representation of life, life force, power, knowledge, divinity, masculine energy, positivity, clarity...

3 The Moon is the symbolic representation of mystery, feminine energy, cyclical change, renewal, transition, mother, love...

Monday arrived, and with it came the long-awaited court appearance. All the offenders were transported from the police department's cells for their hearings at court. It was a daunting sight, with lawbreakers from all departments of Wasteland jam-packed into one cell, faces crushed with apprehension.

The cell gates at court clanged shut, locking them all in.

Suddenly, a gangster let out a fierce and uncompromising cry within the cell, commanding all gang members to rise and ordering everyone else to remain seated.

Luke knew what was expected of him at that moment, but instead of standing up he stayed seated and silent, not uttering a word of their coded language. There was a time when he'd lived with the gangsters in Wasteland and he'd learned a few things about this moment and what he was about to face.

Like ancient warlords seizing the power of opportunity, the gangsters began discussing the rules of excessive pride and social order. Their words were a mishmash of ideas, snakebites and dog-eat-dog mentality, mixed with gangsta rap. They were the kings of bad behaviour in a world of poison, gold, false prophets, crisis and pain.

The gangsters spoke in a language wrapped in secrecy, sealing their world with words only they could understand. Their souls were stranded over a war of east-side and west-side turf.

As Luke sat there, surrounded by criminals, he felt a sense of detachment. It was like watching a movie, observing the chaos and madness, and he knew he couldn't remain on the sidelines forever. He felt the weight of hopelessness settling in as he watched the gangsters. The despair inside him grew deeper and deeper with each passing moment, like a bottomless pit.

The gangsters first held their counsel to find out 'who was who' and everyone's ranking in their crooked order. Luke noticed their twisted expressions as they fought for dominance in a jungle that had no mercy for the weak. He knew that he had to play his cards right if he wanted to survive.

Then a few selected gangsters acting as chief soldiers made their rounds to the criminals seated on the floor, took what they had, and brought it all back to their leader, the boss of the gangsters, who was like a king; his followers were loyal to the bone. Then they began their rituals and offerings of drugs. Needle after needle, their faces contorted with pleasure and pain.

They worshipped a false god of misbehaviour and corruption. This place had no hope, light or redemption – only the constant struggle for power and dominance, where the strongest preyed on the weak.

Luke knew he had to keep his wits about him to survive in this harshness. He couldn't afford to show any weakness or vulnerability. He found himself lost in the chaos, searching the shadows on the walls for answers, his mind unable to navigate the raging waters that threatened to drown him.

Like rolling stones across the threshing floor, the prisoners tumbled one by one, assaulted by the deafening sounds of judgment – to be held in prison or released until trial. Despite the chaos, Luke remained unnoticed by the gangsters for a while, but only until the number of inmates lessened as they went to see the judge. Then, one of the gang members' gaze fell on Luke. Luke knew that the man intended to rob him of his meagre possessions. His mind went blank, and he acted purely on instinct, wiping off his mask, he fixed his gaze on the gangster, demanding to know what he wanted. Without hesitation, the gangster replied, and then Luke stood up, facing him with steeliness. They were nose to nose, and the tension in the air was dense. In a split second, Luke uttered a single word, and the fight erupted.

Luke rained punches on the gangster. In no time, the other gangsters, in a collective force, attacked him from behind, tearing Luke from their now bloodied comrade. This was how the stage was set. The belt appeared, and then the whips, until the gang boss commanded that they stop.

For a while, Luke had lived with the gangsters on the streets of Wasteland. During that time, one of them told him that if he should ever go to prison, he must never allow anyone to take anything that belonged to him. Otherwise, his stay in prison would make him want to kill himself.

Thus, through this course, by such a curriculum, Luke had to do what he had done. Nonetheless, as the gangsters walked away, Luke felt a mix of rage and helplessness.

The court sentenced him to ninety days in prison. And so, he was burdened by time and the confinement of walls, all rights reserved, and he was also denied the keys to the doors in a house of many storeys filled with darkened satisfactions.

Prison was a university of ingeniously devious and dangerous people from whom it appeared there would be no escape. And so, Luke asked a gang member what he needed to do to be initiated as a member. After enquiry was made of the gang boss, he was told that he would get a rusted, broken blade and that Luke must stab a jailer in the neck and bring dark death upon him.

Such is the nature of this case. The road there had been paved with the best intentions.

And so, it seemed there would be little that I could now do.

Yet my son was wrong too, for he did not know about the power of the Moon either.

For me, Mrs Moon, this case was like a myth from a bygone age that I reasoned was not real. I felt deranged and lost at sea as in all classical tragedies. And – as in the tradition of all classical tragedies – poetry, dance and song served as the central backdrop to me for the unfolding of this plot.

Dancing Addiction

Join me in my dance with addiction:
A wild and erratic dance.
I twirled and swayed, a wretched figure
In the grip of a dangerous romance.

I danced in the shadows of Disease,
Its icy fingers, a chilling touch.
But in Darkness I found a glimmer,
A light within that mattered much.

Disharmony, my dance partner,
Threw me off with every move,
But I don't let him bring me under:
I find my beat and keep my groove.

And Darkness, a formidable foe,
Its cloak enveloping me tight.
Yet, in its grasp I found resilience,
A flame burning with undying might.

Through the trials of addiction's sway,
I discovered strength I never knew.
I am a lion, bold and fierce,
Not just a meek and timid ewe.

So come, join me in this new dance,
Where love and joy are the guiding light.
Together we'll twirl, we'll spin and soar,
And revel in the beauty of life's delight.

The Enabler

Will I ever find my rest?
Loneliness is my relentless guest.
My dreams, once bright, now lost in haze,
Every single night, tears mark the endless days.

I'm weary, worn and so, so tired.
In cleaning up his mess, my soul is mired.
By enabling his addiction's grip,
My love for him is a sinking ship.

I provide for him, care for his needs,
Give him money, fulfilling his pleas.
But my heart aches with each sacrifice:
Enabling his habit is a painful vice.

I've made his burden my own to bear.
Shouldering the weight of a constant snare,
I protect my son with lies and deceit,
Hiding the truth, a desperate feat.

My life, once mine, now in disarray,
Revolves around his addiction's sway.
But I know, deep down in my core,
Enabling is not love, but a facade to abhor.

Seeking support, I'll stand up strong,
Reclaiming my worth, where I belong.
I am more than an addiction enabler:
A warrior, a fighter, a truth revealer!

I'll chart my own course, find my way,
Live my life, come what may.
For I deserve to thrive and be free,
No longer chained to codependency.

So, I'll step forward, with courage in my heart,
Setting boundaries, though it may be hard.
With love and compassion, and clarity,
I'll break the chain and set myself free.

Chapter 1

The Shipwreck on the Bay of Falsehood

I felt the weight of exhaustion pressing down on me, leaving me drained and overwhelmed. 'How did I get here? Why is this happening to me? What have I done?'

Lost in the swirling chaos of my mind, the answers eluded me.

My son, my Luke had become a stranger, lost in the grip of addiction. I'd become a liar, hiding the truth from my husband Zach, afraid of what he might do if he knew about all the things Luke had stolen from our home. I feared for Luke's safety, but my anger simmered beneath the surface, threatening to boil over and consume us all.

I held Zach responsible for not being there for Luke when he needed him, preoccupied by his work and oblivious to the creeping signs of addiction in our lives.

At least, that's what I believed.

Our once joyful home now resembled a prison or a mental institution, We were suffocating under the weight of constant fights and tension. The toll it took on us was ravaging, and divorce crossed my mind as a haunting possibility. I was constantly on edge, carrying the keys to all the rooms in our home and keeping everything locked up to prevent Luke from stealing more things to support his habit. He had taken so much already: money, appliances, cutlery, office equipment and things I wouldn't discover for the longest time. I'd tried hiding our belongings, but he always managed to find them.

I devised an idea to deter him from stealing our CDs and DVDs. I wrote my name and phone number on each one with a permanent marker, making it clear that they belonged to me. It was a small act of defiance; a way to protect what little remained of our possessions from Luke's addiction.

But his addiction continued to spiral out of control. He stole my great-grandfather's gold pocket watch, and I was afraid to tell Zach for fear of his violent reaction. I felt helpless, watching Luke wasting away before my eyes, his body and mind ravaged by drugs.

I tried to talk to him, reason with him and make him understand the pain and destruction his addiction was causing our family, but my words fell on deaf ears. At other times, I lost my temper and vented my anger, but it only seemed to push him further away.

Despite everything, I still held on to hope. Zach had bought Luke a guitar for his birthday and he had shown a talent for it, quickly picking up songs after just a few lessons. I imagined a future where our family could be happy and whole, gathered around Luke as he played his guitar, entertaining friends and loved ones.

But that hope was short-lived. Luke sold his guitar for drugs, and my heart broke again. I was alone in my struggle, unable to find help or support from those around me. I continued to lie to my family and friends, making excuses for Luke's behaviour and pretending that everything was fine when it was far from it.

Luke and my precious daughter Alisa were the centre of my universe. I would go to any lengths to safeguard them, and especially Luke, who was now so trapped in that dark grip. I blamed the company he kept, our immoral society, and anything else I could blame to avoid facing the harsh reality. Every time I refused to believe he was an addict, convinced that it was just a phase he was going through.

I wore a smile on my face, but my heart was torn, aching and bleeding. I longed for the day Luke would see the damage he was causing and choose to change his ways. Until then, I would continue to fight for my family, navigating the treacherous waters of addiction and holding on to hope, even as the ship of our lives seemed to be sinking in the bay of false promises.

I continued to put on a facade, pretending that my life was perfect, hoping that no one would see through me and that everyone would believe that everything was fine. I didn't want others to know the turmoil in my life. I wanted my friends and family to think that we were a happy and prosperous family, despite the chaos that Luke's drug-taking had caused.

My worst fears were realised when two policemen banged on the front door one night. We were all fast asleep, except for Luke. He wasn't home. He had been out with his friends and was supposed to have been back hours before. My heart pounded violently against my chest as I hurried down the stairs to open the door, expecting the worst. The policemen informed me that Luke had stolen from someone, though I couldn't remember the name. My brain switched off, stunned by the news.

After that incident, I started getting sick. The first time it happened, I thought I'd had a heart attack and was dying.

My body temperature rose, and my heart started pounding faster, eventually becoming a strangling pain in my chest. I struggled to breathe; each breath would become shallower and quicker. I battled with my body and tried to remove my clothing as sweat poured down me. I ended up lying on the cool tiled floor of the bathroom, trying to cool down. Then everything went black. It took a while before I woke up, still lying on the floor, utterly exhausted.

Lily told me afterwards that she thought I'd had an anxiety attack and suggested I try breathing into a paper bag if it happened again. Well, it did happen again three times after that. I followed Lily's advice, and it helped a bit. But I was still afraid it could happen again, so I made an appointment with my physician. He said it was an anxiety attack, and to my surprise he diagnosed hypertension too.

I constantly made excuses for Luke when people asked where he was and how he was doing. He was often fast asleep in his bed, still feeling the effects of the drugs. But I lied and said that he was tired from working and was taking a nap or was out with his friends when I didn't know where he was. I felt incredibly anxious when friends or family came around, fearing Luke might steal from them, which he had done before. I was embarrassed by his actions. Sometimes, I hid in the bathroom when it all became too much to handle. With the door closed, I felt safe to let my tears flow.

Once I stared into the bathroom mirror. I witnessed the stranger staring back at me with a red face soaked with tears, puffy eyes and a runny nose. Intensely heavy sobs poured from my heart while the thought of getting away from it all rushed through my mind. I tried to control my sobs so that no one would hear me.

I asked Luke what was happening to him but he brushed me off, avoiding my questions and deflecting my concerns. It was like a wall had been built between us, and I couldn't break through to reach my son. I felt helpless and heartbroken, watching him spiral deeper into addiction.

Then I reached out for help, sought advice from friends and family, and even considered therapy for Luke and me. But nothing seemed to work. I felt like a failure as a mother, as if I had somehow failed to protect my son from the clutches of addiction.

The weight of it all was crushing me. I put on a brave face in front of others, pretending everything was okay. But in the solitude of the bathroom I allowed myself to let go and cry, releasing the pent-up frustration, anger and sadness that was inside.

Looking at my reflection in the mirror, I barely recognised myself. The once confident and composed woman had been replaced by someone worn down and defeated. Luke's addiction was taking its toll on me too, and I didn't know how much longer I could keep going on like this.

I knew I needed to take care of myself and find ways to cope and heal from the pain and stress. I couldn't give up on Luke, but I couldn't sacrifice my well-being entirely. It was a difficult balance to strike, but I had to try.

With a deep breath, I wiped away my tears, composed myself and walked out of the bathroom. I made a vow to keep fighting for Luke, to keep trying to reach him, but also to prioritise my own mental and emotional health. I would seek support, find healthy ways to cope, and never give up on the hope that Luke could overcome his addiction and return to being the person I knew he could be.

I felt a glimmer of strength and determination as I closed the door behind me. With love for my family and myself, I was determined to keep going, one step at a time, until we found our way out of this dark and painful chapter in our lives. It wouldn't be easy, but I was willing to face whatever challenges came my way.

What had become of me?

There were moments when I wanted to run away from it all, to escape from the constant worry and heartache. Reading books became my solace, a way to lose myself in fictional worlds and forget, even just for a while, the pain of reality. Sometimes I read for just a few minutes, and other times for hours, finding refuge in the words on the pages.

But even with the distraction of books, I found it difficult to sleep at night. The weight of our plight kept me awake and getting out of bed in the morning felt like an impossible task. I longed to stay in bed and hide from the world, but I had a family to care for and responsibilities that couldn't be ignored.

The stress and emotional toll of Luke's addiction impacted on my physical health. I had no appetite, yet I found myself eating unhealthy snacks during the day and in bed at night, seeking comfort in food. The lack of proper nutrition and sleep caused me to gain weight and dark circles formed around my eyes, a physical reflection of the turmoil I was experiencing inside. There were moments when I wanted to scream, to let out the overwhelming emotions that had built up inside me. But I had to control myself, afraid of the primal, animalistic sound that might escape my lips. I felt like I was barely holding on, trying to keep it together for the sake of my family and Luke.

I wondered what had happened to my sweet, clever little Luke. I couldn't understand why he couldn't see the pain he was causing himself and our family. I questioned why I couldn't change him, despite all the love and effort I had poured into him.

There were moments when I felt utterly overwhelmed, when the weight of life seemed unbearable, and death seemed like a welcome respite.

During those dark times, I felt a deep longing for my mother, wishing I could talk to her, to seek her wisdom and guidance in this difficult time. I longed for her embrace and for her to tell me everything would be alright.

The yearning for my mother grew more intense. It had been a decade since she'd passed on, but the pain felt fresh, as if it had happened yesterday. The emptiness left by her absence never seemed to fade, especially in the quiet moments of sadness.

I longed for the closeness we'd once shared, our talks and laughter that had been a balm for my soul. I yearned for a time when we could be reunited without the strife and heartache that had become my reality. Lately, I had started seeing my mother everywhere – in the things we used to love, in the melodies and lyrics of our favourite songs, in the echoes of her words in what others said. Oh, how I wished I had her unwavering strength.

The ache in my heart grew more acute with this yearning, and death seemed to offer a peaceful escape. I felt vulnerable, unable to bear the weight of her absence any longer. I craved the comfort of her presence, her guidance and her love, as if it could make everything right again.

Chapter 2

Little Ella

A haven of light and joy during the day, our home was overshadowed by my father's dark presence when he came home drunk in the evening on Fridays and Saturdays. The harsh stench of alcohol filled the air as he stumbled through the front door, struggling to keep his balance. I would try to keep my mind steady, but the fear would clutch me tightly.

My mother, a beacon of love and kindness, would rush to the kitchen to fetch my father's food as he barked commands at her, reducing her to a servant. Seeing her being treated so poorly broke my heart and I despised my father for making her feel so small.

She had been the source of my best childhood memories: organising concerts with my siblings and me, playing the judge and making us feel like stars. Her powerful voice singing songs like Barbara Streisand's *Memories* still echoed in my ears, and I had learned them by heart just by listening to her.

My father turned the evenings that were supposed to be filled with laughter and joy into moments of tension and fear. And, despite my mother's contagiously joyful nature, I saw a deep sadness in her eyes during those evenings when my father's drunkenness took over – a stark contrast to her usual vibrant self.

My father's rule was fear, and when under the influence his modus operandi was always the same. He would demand my mother bring his food and she would comply, submitting to his orders like a servant. It was a dreadful reminder of his dominance and control and fuelled my anger towards him. I longed for my mother to stand up to him and break free of his grip, but she seemed trapped in a cycle of fear and resignation.

Despite the challenges at home, my mother exuded love and kindness to everyone around her, extending her passion for life to neighbours, family, friends, and even strangers. Her unwavering resilience and love for us, her children, inspired me. She was my pillar of strength.

I dreaded the evenings after my father's meals. After he'd finished eating, he would summon all the children to his room, and the mere thought of it sent shivers through me. My body would go numb with fear, and all I wanted to do was run away. But we had learned the hard way that defying my father's summons only made things worse. So, with dread and heavy hearts, we would walk robotically to our parents' room, bracing ourselves for what was to come.

As soon as we entered the room, I could feel my body losing control. My father would be lying on his bed, his red eyes glaring at us with a strange sunken look. His facial skin was fleshy and uneven, a testament to years of indulgence and excess. His actions were slow and clumsy, but his temper was legendary and we knew better than to provoke him. He would speak in a harsh, antagonistic voice, asking us, 'So, what do you have to tell me?'

We would remain silent, too afraid to respond, as we had learned that whatever we said would be used against us. We would stare at my father with wide, fearful eyes, trying to gauge a response. He would then instruct us to remove his shoes and socks, which were sweaty and smelly from a day's wear. With disgust and fear, we did as he commanded, doing our best to hide our revulsion.

While we were busy with this task, my father would slur how dim, dumb and ignorant we were. His words would cut deep, leaving wounds that would fester long after I left home. The scars were emotional and psychological, affecting each of us in different ways. He would dismiss us with a curt, 'Go and sleep now,' and we would leave his room heavy hearted, with a sense of defeat.

Those deep scars shaped my perception of myself for years. I grew up believing I was inferior and that everyone else was better than me. His words were a poison, robbing me of my self-worth and confidence. I often cried myself to sleep, hoping in sleep to escape the suffocating grip of my father's tyranny.

Despite the darkness that loomed over my childhood, there were also many moments of joy and love.

I do remember too how my mother and my father would play with us. They would switch on the radio and sing and dance for us, encouraging us to join in. The melodies and laughter would fill the room, temporarily lifting the heavy cloud that hung over us.

Sometimes our Daddy came home with a special treat: a bag of chocolates. As soon as we caught a whiff of the rich cocoa aroma, our eyes would light up with excitement. We would gather around the coffee table, eager to indulge. With tender care, we would peel back the glossy paper of each chocolate, savouring each morsel: the tangy sensation of the cherry-filled chocolates, the rich buttery sweetness of the caramel ones, and the nutty crunch of the hazelnut pralines, as if it held the key to our happiness. In those moments, we could forget about the darkness lurking just around the corner, lost in the sheer delight of the rich, velvety flavours that danced on our tongues. Time stopped as we indulged in the simple pleasure of these treats. It was in these small, cherished moments that we found solace from the troubles that lurked beyond, creating a cocoon of warmth and happiness that enveloped us.

And then there were also the vibrant wrappers. Each chocolate was encased in a translucent cloak of brilliant blue, lush green, sunny yellow or fiery red. The colours seemed to come alive, adding an extra layer of enchantment to the already irresistible allure of the chocolates. We would gather them and see life through the lens of those colourful wrappers – a world full of imagination and childlike wonder. But it wasn't just about the chocolates. It was about the time we spent together as a family. Our Daddy decided which board game and we would settle in for a friendly round. We laughed and shared stories as we played, enjoying each other's company and creating cherished memories.

Those chocolate-filled evenings with Daddy were magical. They were moments of pure joy, where worries melted away. The taste of the chocolates lingered, yet the warmth of Daddy's love and the laughter etched the sweetest impression in our hearts.

It was during those moments that I would briefly forget the harsh reality of my father's reign of terror.

Our Mummy was a master storyteller. She would captivate us with tales of her childhood, growing up in poverty after losing her mother at a young age. Her stories were a tapestry of her life, woven with threads of hardships and challenges, interlaced with moments of unwavering resilience, heartwarming humour, boundless love and unshakable hope.

One particular story that Mummy often told us was about her mother, our grandmother. Despite her strict demeanour, she was always laughing and singing. She instilled the values of respect, compassion and inner strength in Mummy. Through her stories, Mummy showed us that we were not defined by our circumstances but by our choices and actions. Her stories painted a picture of resilience and love, always filling my heart with warmth. She taught us to believe in ourselves and our uniqueness, even in times of adversity.

Our home was filled with books, instilling in me a deep appreciation for the written word. Daddy would captivate us with the tale of his grandfather's precious pocket watch, carefully kept in a beautifully carved wooden box in his bedroom cupboard. Those stories ignited my love for books and reading at an early age, a passion my parents wholeheartedly fostered.

Immersed in the pages of countless books, I found comfort in a world of fantasy where I could be anything I wanted to be. Enchanted princesses, daring adventurers and noble knights were my constant companions as I delved into the realms of imagination.

Daddy's creativity and perfectionism inspired me, and he taught us various skills, including crafting our toys. Despite not having much money, our home was brimming with endless activities that kept us happily engaged.

Our days were filled with simple joys. With Daddy's guidance and assistance, we crafted kites that danced and soared high in the boundless sky and built carts that raced down the hills, fuelled by our youthful enthusiasm and imagination. Under the warmth of the sun, we laughed and played, pouring our hearts into our creations. We learned the importance of patience, precision and perseverance as we worked side by side, honing our skills as days went by.

When our kites took flight, we held our breath, eyes fixed on the colourful patterns that painted the sky. Those were magical moments, as our creations danced with the wind, reaching for the heavens. And when we rode our handmade carts down the hills, we felt the wind in our faces and the adrenaline pumping through our veins. With Daddy's expertise, we learned to navigate the twists and turns, feeling the rush of excitement as we raced against each other, fuelled by the sheer joy of the ride. We fashioned intricate paper balls and dolls with handmade clothing, constructing catapults, indulging in drawings and paintings. The world was a treasure trove of excitement and learning that I embraced with boundless curiosity.

In the quiet moments, I would gaze at the ceiling, envisioning myself walking upside-down in the house or pondering the mysteries of the night sky from our balcony, counting the stars and wondering about the universe. As night descended, I would lie in bed, eyes narrowed, focusing on the soft glow of the light bulb. I was captivated by the enchanting display of speckled and swirling golden dust as it danced in the warm glow above my bed. I watched, spellbound by the graceful movements and the mesmerising play of colours. It felt like a moment of pure magic, a fleeting beauty that left me entranced and lost in wonder.

It was a nightly ritual that brought me endless joy and wonder. Mummy would sometimes caution me, warning that I might strain my eyes or even risk blindness by staring at the light for too long. But I couldn't tear my gaze away. The allure of the golden-speckled dust held me captive, as if it held the secrets of the universe within its tiny particles.

I had always felt different from other children. While they played and laughed, I often found myself lost in daydreams, a world of my creation where I could reshape reality as I pleased. In these dreams, I crafted a world that reflected my deepest desires, where everyone was content, and troubles melted away like ice in the sun. There was no fighting, no screaming and no pain to be found. Instead, there were songs of birds and conversations with animals and plants. I soared over majestic mountains, traversed vast oceans and ventured to distant planets. Nothing was unattainable in this realm and my imagination knew no bounds.

During my primary school years, I often found myself lost in daydreams, much to the distress of my teacher. I remember hearing her voice calling out, 'Ella, wake up!' as I snapped back to reality, realising that once again I had drifted off in class.

As a result, my academic performance was average, since my mind would often wander. I recall one particular instance when my teacher stood at the front of the classroom, delivering a lesson, but my mind had taken me to a serene meadow with lush, green grass, vibrant flowers and towering trees casting cool shadows by a babbling river. It was a place where I could sing, dance, run free, bask in the warm sun and breathe in the fresh air. 'Ella!' I heard my teacher's distant and stern voice. 'You are daydreaming again. Can you please tell me the answer?'

I stammered, embarrassed and meek. 'I… I don't know, Miss.'

Her soft yet reproachful tone made me feel even more self-conscious, and the laughter of my classmates only added to my discomfort. I felt a lump in my throat, was on the verge of tears. I couldn't comprehend why some of my peers found it amusing to laugh at my expense when I was feeling so down. It hurt deeply and I struggled to understand why they would derive joy from my embarrassment. Despite my best efforts to stay focused, daydreaming seemed to have a hold on me, and I wished I could shake it off and be fully present in class. The experience left me feeling vulnerable and isolated, longing for understanding and empathy from my classmates and teachers alike.

The years passed, I turned sixteen, but my father's alcoholism continued to haunt our home. Every Friday and Saturday evening, he would stumble in drunk, ruling our household with fear. I couldn't understand why my mother stayed with him, enduring his disrespect, the fear-inducing behaviour and outbursts that even the neighbours could hear. We were all afraid of him when he was in that state. I promised myself that I would never marry someone like him: someone who would make me feel frightened, bully me and embarrass me in front of others.

One Saturday evening, a boy from my class came to visit. It was around eight o'clock when my father arrived home, and he chased the boy out of the house, asserting that he should have asked for permission to visit. The incident devastated me and the boy started ignoring me at school. I solemnly vowed that I would never allow any boys to come to my house again.

As I lay in bed, tears streaming down my face, I prayed for change and guidance to end this nightmare.

Chapter 3

At Work

Nadia, my dear colleague and friend at Benny's Bookstore, expressed her concern for me with a touch of sympathy in her voice. 'You shouldn't worry so much, Ella,' she said, her eyes filled with compassion. 'You look worn out. I'm sure this is just a teenage phase that Luke is going through. Your children will be okay. You are the perfect mother.'

I had confided in Nadia about my growing suspicions regarding Luke's behaviour. He seemed distant, avoiding eye contact and immersing himself in heavy metal music that grated on my nerves. The relentless loudness and aggressiveness of it all had taken over our home, suffocating me and making the air feel heavy and oppressive. I had repeatedly asked him to turn off the blaring radio, raising my voice in frustration before he complied. To make matters worse, he'd started wearing his pants hanging low on his hips like a gangster, and I constantly had to remind him to pull them up.

Nadia's words of reassurance echoed in my mind: 'Ella, don't worry. You are the perfect mother.' I wanted to believe her, but doubts gnawed at me. With all my heart I hoped this was just a fleeting phase, something Luke would outgrow in time.

As a devoted mother, I worked only the morning shift at Benny's Bookstore near our home, a perfect arrangement that allowed me to be home when Luke and Alisa returned from school. Working at Benny's also came with the perk of having access to a wide range of books and information resources, both old and new. It was a valuable opportunity for me, especially since I had begun to suspect that Luke might be involved in drugs. I delved into as many books on addiction as possible, determined to arm myself with knowledge.

After my shift, I would dive into housework and cooking, ensuring that our home was tidy and that a warm meal awaited my children. I took pride in helping Luke and Alisa with their homework and school projects, always making time to sit down and provide guidance. Our family had a strict routine: supper promptly at six and the kids in bed by eight o'clock. However, since Luke had started high school, bedtime had been pushed to nine o'clock, a concession I made to accommodate his changing schedule.

Little did I know that these seemingly ordinary routines would soon be disrupted by a series of events that would challenge me as a mother in ways I'd never imagined.

Most of the things in my life were going according to plan. I was a master of organisation, diligently writing down my daily schedule in the mornings to create order and structure. It allowed me to pursue my passions of painting and dance, finding solace in the creative outlets that brought me joy. Zach and I were united in our desire to provide the best possible life for our children. He cared for our finances while I nurtured our home with love and care.

Like any married couple, we had our fair share of obstacles and disagreements along the way. From minor squabbles to more serious discussions about finances and parenting decisions, we faced our challenges head-on. However, despite these hurdles, our commitment to our family always prevailed. We knew that no relationship was perfect, and ours was no exception. We had our differences, our unique quirks, and occasional misunderstandings. There were moments when we didn't see eye to eye, and our emotions sometimes got the better of us. But what set us apart was our unwavering determination to find common ground and work through our issues together, to make our family work. We had faced our fair share of challenges, both big and small, but we had never encountered any that we couldn't overcome. We had weathered financial setbacks, health scares and moments of doubt, but we always managed to come out stronger on the other side.

And so, we persevered, always keeping in mind the bigger picture: our shared dreams, our love for our children and our commitment to the family.

We were proud of the life we had built together.

As I flipped through the family album, filled with photos of Alisa and Luke's innocent smiles and carefree laughter, I felt a pang of sadness. Despite my pride in Alisa, I found myself unable to spend as much time with her as I wanted to, as my life became consumed by Luke's distressing behaviour. It was heartbreaking to experience Luke's mood swings, rebellion and detachment from the family. The teenage years had hit Luke hard, and our challenges seemed insurmountable.

I was always there for my children, providing love, support and guidance. But Luke's addiction was something I had never anticipated. I had done everything I could to create a nurturing and loving environment for my children, yet addiction had found its way into our lives, affecting us all.

I questioned myself incessantly. What had I done wrong? Was I not attentive enough? Had I missed any signs? I was consumed by guilt and self-doubt. But I knew I couldn't afford to lose hope.

I realised that, despite our challenges, there were still so many things to be grateful for: a supportive family, loyal friends and a deep-rooted love for my children that would never waver.

I vowed to remain committed to my children, no matter how tough it got.

Amid my turmoil, I found solace in my mother's teachings. I drew strength from her unwavering resolve to face challenges. She had met her share of hardships with grace and courage, and I was determined to do the same, although I did not know how.

Chapter 4

The Crisis

It was a sunny afternoon, and I had asked Luke and his friend to close the door behind them as they went out to play soccer in front of our home. I prepared sandwiches and tea in the kitchen. About ten minutes later all was ready and I went outside to call them in. But they were nowhere to be found. A sense of unease crept into my stomach, and I knew something wasn't right.

I hurried back inside the house to see if they had returned, but they were not there. Panic rose as I feared the worst. Determined to find them, I decided to search the neighbourhood. It didn't take long before I spotted them, two blocks from our home.

As I approached them, I saw Luke and his friend smoking. They were standing in a narrow alley between two houses, and the pungent smell of weed filled the air. Anger boiled up inside me as I looked at my stunned son with his crimson face. No words came out of his open mouth.

'What are you two doing?' I asked angrily, my legs shaky with emotion. Luke remained silent, and I felt the weight of disappointment bore down on me. 'Let's go home. I'll talk to your dad when he gets home later.'

I turned to Luke's friend, my voice as calm as I could make it. 'Please never come to our house again. Consider yourself no longer friends with Luke.'

In that moment, I placed the blame on Luke's friend. Anger and determination surged as I vowed to do whatever it took to save Luke. My heart ached with the realisation that my child had succumbed to drugs, and I was determined to make choices for him if he couldn't make them for himself.

Luke's drug use turned my world upside-down. I felt exhausted, constantly on edge, and overcome by the need to monitor his every move like a security guard.

But then things took an even darker turn.

The first time I discovered money missing from my purse, which I always kept in my bedroom, is burned into my memory. When I confronted Luke, he casually shrugged it off, saying, 'I was in the kitchen eating since I came home. I was never in your bedroom, Mom.'

I felt disoriented, torn between wanting to believe him and the overwhelming evidence pointing to the fact that he was stealing from me and lying about it. How could my son, whom I had raised with morals and ethics, become a thief and a liar?

It was a devastating blow.

As time went on, the situation only worsened. Things started disappearing from our home and I found myself in constant confusion and disbelief, too afraid to confront Luke directly, always hoping against hope that it wasn't him. I couldn't fathom how this could happen to me, a mother who had given her best to her family.

Despite the chaos and turmoil that became a constant, I was determined to keep my family together. I knew I had to try to understand what Luke was going through to prevent him from getting into even more trouble. It was relentless:

the battle to reconcile the image of the son I thought I knew, with the reality of his actions. But I had resolved to do whatever it took to help him.

During Luke's ninth grade, the principal called for a meeting with Zach and me. We sat anxiously in his office, listening to him explain that Luke had been keeping company with the wrong crowd and had been caught smoking marijuana with them. The principal expressed his concern and had decided to warn Luke, hoping it would set him on the right path.

Zach and I were devastated. We couldn't believe that our son had fallen so far and into such bad company. We blamed his friends for leading him astray and decided to take action.

We made the difficult decision to change Luke's school. We opted for a school with smaller class sizes, deciding that, in smaller classes he would receive individual attention and have a better chance at turning his life around. We were hopeful too that the change in environment would help Luke break away from his addiction and positively change his life. However, Luke's addiction continued, despite our efforts. It caused more and more friction in our family, and we struggled to understand why Luke was going down this destructive path.

His once vibrant personality seemed to have faded, and he appeared ever more distant. I tried conversations with Luke, asking him about school and how he was feeling, but he most often brushed me off, insisting that everything was fine. However, to my dismay, I was well aware that it wasn't.

As Luke's exam results continued to decline, my concern grew even stronger. I started to pay closer attention to his behaviour and habits. I noticed changes in his demeanour, his sleep patterns and his overall attitude towards school. It became apparent to me that Luke was struggling with something beyond just academic challenges.

I wondered if Luke was grappling with an underlying stress and anxiety. The thought of him turning to harmful behaviours was distressing.

Then we received a call from the new principal towards the end of the third term when Luke was in Grade 12. We were asked to come immediately to the school and were perplexed to learn that Luke had been absent for three consecutive days, including that day. It was hard to believe, as he had been leaving home every morning to go to school. The principal had also called Luke's classmates to the office. They said that they had seen the police picking him up outside the school premises after they'd found marijuana in his possession.

My worst fear was creeping up on me: the possibility of Luke being jailed. I strongly suspected that Luke was acting out when his exam marks plummeted drastically. He was no longer the bright student he once was. Zach and I immediately drove to the nearest police station and found Luke sitting in a cell like a convict. The policeman on duty was friendly and allowed Luke to be released with a warning, as it was his first offence.

So, the following day and until his last day of school, I accompanied Luke to school to ensure he attended every day. I was determined to see him pass his exams and have a chance at university, as I wanted my children to be educated, successful, independent and happy.

While I waited for Luke in the school's reception area, I read the book I'd brought along. I'd made arrangements at work to take time off on the days he had exams, to ensure that he didn't get into any more trouble. I hoped he would change once he started attending university the following year. He would be older and would hopefully outgrow this reckless teenage phase.

Chapter 5

Dreams

Zach and I shared a vision for our children's futures. We aimed to provide unwavering support to our offspring in pursuing their chosen careers. We recognised that our children had unique talents and interests that could lead them on different paths, and we were committed to embracing their individuality. Above all, our ultimate goal was to empower them to achieve their full potential and find fulfilment in their adult lives.

At age five, Luke showed a keen interest in piracy, inspired by his beloved *Pirate Boy* book. To encourage his imagination, I'd gifted him a pirate costume and a toy sword, which he'd wielded with great enthusiasm. Luke's aspirations evolved as he grew older, from wanting to become a teacher in his early school years to a dream of being a doctor or accountant. By the time he reached Grade 10, he was set on pursuing a career as an actuary, drawn to its potential earnings.

Alisa, Luke's sister, was a joyous and delightful child whose name, which means happy, perfectly suited her cheerful demeanour. Her infectious laughter and radiant smile could brighten up any room. Despite her sensitivity, Alisa had impressive resilience and could bounce back quickly, even after experiencing brief moments of sadness. She developed a keen interest in psychology and interior design in Grade 6. As Luke's struggles with drug addiction worsened, I struggled to balance my responsibilities between being there for Alisa and supporting Luke. The daily stress of his drug abuse, his lies and the gradual disappearance of our belongings became all-consuming, leaving little room for happy memories. My heart yearned for the days when Alisa and I had laughed until tears streamed down our faces and our stomachs ached from pure joy.

In recent times, Luke's absence during our family gatherings had been apparent. He preferred spending time with his friends or keeping to himself, often turning down our invitations to join us at the dining table. Whenever people asked me about him, I felt a pang of embarrassment, as I was unsure of his whereabouts.

His sudden arrival in the wee hours of the morning left me worried and sick. His red eyes and intoxicated state made me furious. Still, I refrained from saying anything and decided to talk to him the following day when he was sober.

Despite putting my family first, I was at a loss for answers.

Why was this happening to me? Why was I being punished?

These questions weighed heavily, as I struggled to find the desperately needed answers.

At my wit's end, I decided to seek help by joining a support group for families in addiction.

I arrived at the meeting a little late, having spent a few minutes trying to locate the venue. As I entered the room, I saw a tall, thin woman starting to speak, introducing herself as Amanda. The group responded with a collective,'Hi, Amanda'. I quietly joined the circle of attendees as we all focused on Amanda as she continued to share her story.

She spoke about her eighteen-year-old daughter, who had been missing for three days. Amanda's friends had reported seeing her on the main road, wearing dirty clothes. She said she couldn't sleep at night, consumed with worry for her daughter who had taken all her money and disappeared. Amanda had been searching for her since she'd left, with no luck.

After Amanda, an older man named Clive shared his story. His son, Ben, was an addict who had lived with him and his wife. Clive had thrown him out of the house many times, but Ben always returned, begging for food. Clive said he couldn't bear to see his children go to bed hungry, so he gave Ben food and a place to sleep but nothing else.

As others shared their stories, I read the leaflet that I'd picked up from the chair before I sat down. It stated, 'Addiction is a chronic disease. It cannot be cured, but it can be managed.' My body went numb with shock. Was this to be my life now, attending meeting after meeting? Was I destined to be a part of this group of 'lunatics' and 'losers'? I didn't belong here. I didn't want to be here. I wanted someone to tell me how to get my life back to normal again.

'Please help me!' my mind screamed silently. 'My son is not like them. He's not an addict.' But deep inside, I knew the truth. I was here because of my son's addiction, and I needed to face that reality if I wanted to help him and myself.

So, I went back to the group the following week. I hoped to hear stories of triumph and transformation instead of the usual tales of despair and heartbreak. After four people had shared their stories, it was my turn. I knew the process by then, so I shared my experience of the week.

'Luke, my nineteen-year-old son, is out on the street. I don't know where he is. I asked him to leave on Monday after he had stolen his sister's tablet. I came here to find out how to deal with him. He has been stealing our things and always returned after a while, begging me to give him food and promising to change. I've taken him back several times, but he has stolen again and again, and continued with his drug abuse.'

Everyone else shared their story of despair.

After the meeting, we sat down for some tea and biscuits. As the conversation flowed, I found myself drawn to Clive. He had a kind face and a gentle manner, and I could sense that he had been through many struggles.

When we were finally alone, I approached him and asked how long he had attended the support group. He told me that he had been coming for eight years and that the group had been his lifeline during some of his darkest moments. He said that he was now the chairman of the group.

I noticed a deep sense of camaraderie and support among the group members. As we talked, Clive opened up more about his son Ben, who had been battling addiction since he was sixteen. Clive's wife had given up on Ben, but Clive refused to let go of hope. He was determined to help his son in any way he could, no matter how long it took.

Hearing Clive's story, I couldn't help but feel a deep sense of sadness and empathy for him and his family. It was clear that the road to recovery was long and challenging and that not everyone could take it.

As I left the meeting, I reflected on my situation with Luke. While the group provided a sense of community and support, I realised it might not be the best fit for me.

I wanted to break free from the cycle of addiction and reclaim my life. I wanted to learn how to overcome my struggles and build a better future for myself and my family.

I wanted to hear stories of change and victory. I had heard none.

Then Luke came back home again, promising me he would change.

I was hesitant to attend another family support group meeting when an old friend invited me to another group. He promised it would be different from my previous experience.

As we walked into the meeting, I was surprised to see some familiar faces, including my former high school teacher, Mr Davids. I couldn't believe he was there, but as he shared his story of his son's addiction, I realised that addiction doesn't discriminate.

The meeting took a dark turn when a woman shared the heartbreaking news of her friend's son, who had overdosed while in rehab. It was a sobering moment, and shook me to the core. I realised that Luke's addiction could lead to his death at any moment. I sat in silence throughout the meeting, taking in the stories of the other attendees. As I left the meeting, I couldn't shake the feeling that, if rehabilitation couldn't help addicts, my family was doomed.

Despite my doubts and fears, I knew I couldn't give up on Luke and our dreams. I had to keep trying, fighting and seeking resources and support to help Luke overcome his addiction.

Chapter 6

The Questions

During this time of fear and confusion, I couldn't make any sense of my life. I lost all sense of meaning and I questioned everything about my life.

I used to believe that if I were respectful, truthful and kind, only good things would happen to me.

So why was my life filled with so many challenges every single day?

Why was it so difficult? What had I done wrong?

I had raised my children with morals and ethics and had a good relationship with them. So, what else could I do, or how could I guide them?

As I grappled with these questions, more appeared in my head.

Who am I?

What am I?

How have I gotten here?

Why am I here?

What is my purpose in life?

These were big, existential questions that I had never really thought about before. But now, in the midst of my agony, they seemed of utmost importance. I spent countless hours pondering these questions, trying to understand my life and place in the world. I didn't know where to turn for answers. I felt lost and alone, as if no one could understand what I was going through.

As I continued to grapple with these questions, I explored different spiritual and philosophical traditions. I read books, searched the internet and spoke with people from different walks of life. Slowly but surely, I began to piece together a deeper understanding of myself and my place in the world.

I learned that my struggles were not unique and that everyone goes through difficult times. I saw them as an invitation to keep exploring, growing, and creating my path in life.

This was the time when my friend Norma invited me to an inspirational talk nearby, and I eagerly accepted the invitation. As we arrived, we found Abu, a middle-aged man, already engrossed in a conversation with a small gathering of about twelve people. He warmly greeted us and asked us to introduce ourselves before resuming his discourse. He confidently stated that each of us is accountable for everything that happens in our lives, whether we realise it or not. This statement perplexed me, and I wondered, 'How could I be responsible for my son's addiction? What have I done wrong?'

Abu's words held my attention when he expressed that we are spiritual beings having a human experience rather than the other way around. This perspective resonated deeply with me, and I became more invested in the discussion. Throughout the evening, he delved into various topics, such as universal laws, quantum physics, and entropy – concepts that were entirely new to me and yet so fascinating.

Abu proposed that we could transform our lives by merely changing our thoughts. He also offered to lead a group meditation the following week, which I eagerly anticipated.

Walking away from the meeting, I felt invigorated and enthused by this new community of individuals, particularly Abu and his unconventional approach.

For the first time, I felt a glimmer of hope that I could improve my circumstances by altering my mindset.

The encounter broadened my horizons and empowered me to seize control of my life. It was like a light bulb switched on in my head. I felt I had the power to create a better life. I felt a sense of excitement and possibility, knowing that a path to a better life was available to me.

This new-found optimism was a turning point for me. It opened my mind to new ideas and perspectives, and I felt inspired to take action to improve my situation. I began to examine my thoughts and beliefs more closely. I sought out ways to cultivate a more positive and growth-oriented mindset.

Chapter 7

Doubts

The universal laws opened up a new world of understanding to me, illuminating concepts that have remained unchanged throughout history. The principles of oneness, attraction, polarity, relativity and cause and effect – all of these captivated my interest. I eagerly shared what I had learned with my family and friends. However, Luke was disinterested.

Despite Zach's best efforts to reach out to Luke, he showed no interest in turning his life around. Luke had flunked all his exams at the university and it seemed confirmed that he were heading down a path of self-destruction.

Zach searched the internet for a solution and discovered a religious school offering educational opportunities for young men over 1 500 kilometres away. Excited about the possibilities, Zach applied on Luke's behalf, and we were all overjoyed when he was accepted.

We felt that at eighteen years old, Luke was finally on the path to realising his potential.

As we waved him goodbye, we prayed that Luke would thrive and become the son we had hoped he could be. Months passed, and we decided to visit him at the school.

Our relief was immense when his teacher reported that Luke was doing well and we saw how happy and healthy he looked. It was an answer to our prayers, and we returned home with renewed optimism for his future.

A month passed and then one morning, while I was cooking, the doorbell rang. To my surprise, I found Luke standing outside with a younger boy. He had run away from school and hiked all the way to our home. Luke begged us not to send him back, fearing punishment from the school. He claimed to have changed and promised never to do drugs again. He said he missed us dearly.

Feeling baffled, I hoped Luke had indeed turned over a new leaf. Zach immediately called the school to inform them of the situation. He arranged to return the younger boy to the school the following day. Thankfully, the school decided not to pursue any further action against Luke.

With nothing to do, Luke spent most of his time at home, and we were worried that he would fall back into old habits. I reached out to people for a support group for recovering addicts. Eventually, I found one that seemed like a good fit for Luke. He started attending their meetings and seemed to be doing well. It was heartening to see him forge connections with other recovering addicts and refer to them as his brothers.

Zach advised Luke to find a job and keep himself occupied during the day.

After a month, Luke landed a job at a call centre in the city. He seemed to thrive at his new workplace and we were proud of him for taking this step towards a more stable future. However, our hopes were short-lived. Just three months into the job, Luke was caught doing drugs in the bathroom.

It was devastating to see him relapse and again, we were all at a loss as to what to do next.

Chapter 8

Rehabilitation Centre

Luke confessed to his manager that he was struggling with drug addiction. His empathetic and supportive manager arranged for Luke to go to a rehabilitation centre for proper treatment and support.

However, I received a call from Luke a week after being admitted, complaining about the poor living conditions and lack of good food at the rehab centre. Despite feeling sorry for him, I consulted with the counsellor and learned that Luke's claims were untrue. With this knowledge, Zach and I decided to leave him at the rehab centre to continue with his treatment.

Days later, Luke ran away from the rehab centre and returned home. He pleaded with me to let him return home, promising to change his ways. Out of love and compassion, I allowed him to come back home. However, Luke ended up losing his call centre job because he hadn't completed the rehab programme, and this left him jobless and struggling to cope.

To ensure Luke stayed on track with his recovery, Zach and I decided to restrict his movements and prevented him from going outdoors. I continued playing the role of security guard more fiercely, hoping he wouldn't take our possessions. Still, it wasn't long before things started disappearing again. My mind felt jumbled most of the time.

One day, Luke announced that he had a job interview and begged us to let him go. We reluctantly agreed, warning him that this was his last chance to prove that he was serious about getting his life back on track.

He left early the following morning.

Then Alisa came to tell me her cell phone was missing.

Days went by, and we didn't hear anything from Luke. As the days turned into weeks, we became increasingly worried. We tried calling him, but his phone was switched off. In the meantime, I discovered more things missing at home that I hadn't been aware had been taken.

One evening, Zach and I had just returned home from a night out with friends. Zach went to the kitchen and I went to our bedroom upstairs. As I climbed the stairs, I noticed a breeze coming from one of the rooms. To my surprise, the office door was open, although I distinctly remembered closing it before we'd left. The lights that had been off had also been switched on. Growing increasingly worried, I removed my shoes and quietly returned downstairs to inform Zach.

Whispering nervously, I said, 'I think someone is upstairs. The office door is open.'

Zach remained calm and composed, despite my growing anxiety. He slowly ascended the stairs, keeping his senses sharp for signs of danger. I trailed behind him, fearfully anticipating the worst.

To our relief, there was no sound except for the gentle breeze from the office. Zach stepped inside and noticed the open window, causing the curtains to move softly back and forth. No one was in the room. However, we soon discovered that our printer and laminator were missing.

Just then, we heard a knock on the front door. Zach went downstairs to answer it and found our neighbour, Captain

Adam, a police captain, waiting for us. Captain Adam had noticed our car in the driveway. He had come over to inform us that he had seen Luke outside our home, carrying equipment in his hands. However, when the captain had tried to approach him, Luke had quickly disappeared.

The incident left us uneasy and unsure of what to make of Luke's sudden reappearance at our home. Nevertheless, we couldn't ignore that he had been involved in the theft.

As time passed, we started receiving letters in the post for Luke. They were from two clothing stores and a medical doctor. The letters sat in the kitchen cupboard for weeks. Eventually, my curiosity got the better of me, and I decided to open them. I was shocked that Luke had purchased expensive clothing brands on one account, including a black leather jacket, two pairs of men's trousers, two white shirts and two T-shirts. The medical account was for a consultation and tablets, for which his medical aid had refused to pay.

I felt a wave of frustration and disappointment. 'Have you ever seen Luke wearing these items?' I asked Zach when he came home from work. Zach couldn't recall seeing him wearing them either. The whole thing made no sense.

As if that weren't enough, a few days later, I was abruptly awoken by loud banging on our front door in the early hours of the morning. It was around two o'clock, and I had been in a deep sleep. As I looked out the window, I saw two police officers standing outside our front door, shouting, 'It's the police! Open up!'

I was terrified and felt my heart was about to explode. With my head spinning, I hurried down the stairs to open the door. Each step felt like a lifetime, and I knew that the officers had come with bad news about Luke.

When I finally reached the door and opened, they asked me if Luke was home. One police officer told me he'd broken into some business and had stolen electronic items. I was so embarrassed and angry with Luke, yet at the same time I was worried about what would happen to him. Depleted and with jumping nerves, I told the police officers that Luke didn't live with us anymore, and they left.

The whole incident left me feeling rattled and on edge.

Chapter 9

Social Assistance

'Hi Ella, it's me, Aunt Sophie.' My aunt's voice sounded composed through the phone. 'I have Luke with me.'

'Oh no,' I groaned as my heart sank. Luke had been spiraling out of control for months.

'He has just showered,' Aunt Sophie continued. 'I gave him fresh clothes from William to wear. I saw him sitting outside my house in filthy clothes. He asked me for something to eat, saying he hadn't eaten for two days. He said he knew he had disappointed the family and wanted to change.'

'Please, Aunt Sophie, don't let him stay there. I'm afraid he might steal from you,' I pleaded, my voice trembling.

'Please take him back. He's our family. I'll only let go of him if you take him back.' Aunt Sophie begged me to reconsider. She sympathised with Luke's plight and didn't want to turn him away. In the end, too embarrassed to allow him to stay with her, I relented and allowed him to come home again.

The situation with Luke had deteriorated and I knew we needed help. A friend suggested we go to Social Services, so the next day, Zach, Luke and I set off to the office. The social worker we met with was young and vibrant, and she was very positive and supportive. 'You need to open up a case against Luke and list everything he stole from you,' she advised. 'Please also describe how his drug abuse affected your household on this form. I will make an application for him to be admitted to rehab. The process can take up to three months.'

I remembered some of the items he'd stolen from us from the twenty-page list I'd received from the second-hand shop I went to after Luke had left with Alisa's cell phone. I'd wanted to find out if he'd sold Alisa's cell phone to them and found out much more than I wanted to know.

I wrote on the form, 'Leather-bound books, electrical food processor, electrical blender, silver cutlery, stainless steel cutlery, gold pocket watch, daughter's tablet and cell phone, printer, laminator...'

It was painful.

As I wrote, I felt a sinking sadness and sense of frustration. I couldn't believe our own son had taken so much from us.

But I also felt a glimmer of hope. Maybe, just maybe, this would be the turning point we needed to get Luke the help he so desperately needed.

While we waited for the state rehab's admission letter, Luke started an outpatient rehabilitation programme near our home. After attending the programme for three weeks, he disappeared again. He was back on the street when we received the call to say that there was an opening for him at the state rehabilitation centre.

Chapter 10

The State Rehabilitation Centre

Zach went out searching for Luke after a friend told him he'd spotted him on the streets of a neighbouring suburb. Zach eventually found him there, strolling along the road. After convincing him to come home, Zach assisted him with bathing and packing his bags before taking him away to rehab.

After a few weeks, we were granted permission to visit. We eagerly took the opportunity to show our support. We wanted to show Luke that we still loved and cared about him, despite our struggles. To accomplish this, we brought him special treats and clothing that we hoped would lift his spirits and make him feel more comfortable. The gifts were meant to serve as a token of our affection and to let him know that we were in his corner, no matter what.

During our visit to Luke, I noticed that many other families had also brought gifts for their recovering loved ones. Their bags were loaded with many delicacies, from snacks and sweets to clothing and other items. It was clear that the families were eager to show their support and to help their relative or friend feel as comfortable as possible during their recovery.

Regrettably, Luke didn't appear particularly thrilled with the gifts we had brought him, causing me to question whether he felt they were inadequate compared to the gifts of other families. There wasn't much conversation between us during the visit. It's possible that he was still struggling with his addiction or feeling overwhelmed by the situation. Whatever the case, the visit was relatively quiet and uneventful, and we eventually had to leave when the visiting hours ended.

Upon returning home, I delved deeper into researching the role of enablers and codependents in addiction. The more I read, the more I recognised how much we had enabled Luke's continuing destructive habits. It was a painful realisation, but I knew we had to stop enabling him so he could recover.

The following week, we arrived empty-handed when we visited Luke at the rehab. He wasn't pleased with our lack of gifts, and it cast a shadow over our time there. There was little conversation before visiting hours were over.

However, the rehab invited us to a family meeting with their social worker, which we attended.

The room was stark, with faded yellow walls and a circle of plastic chairs. The social worker spoke to us about the effects of addiction on families and asked us how Luke's addiction had affected us.

Zach spoke up first, expressing his frustration with the situation. 'I've done everything I could, yet he continued using drugs. Luke has been to other rehabs before but never completed their programme. I hope he told us the truth and will complete the programme here now.'

I was unable to speak, overwhelmed by emotions and tears. Alisa was also sobbing heavily next to me, unable to articulate her thoughts.

After a few more weeks, Luke completed the programme and came home. Physically, he looked healthy and I felt a sense of joy in my heart. However, I was unsure of how to treat him. While he quickly found a job, he soon started using his earnings for drugs again.

At this point, I realised I couldn't trust him and asked him to leave home until he sorted himself out. It was a tough decision, but I knew it was the only way for Luke to recognise the severity of his addiction and start taking responsibility for his own life.

Despite our difficulties, I hoped and prayed that he would be able to turn his life around.

Chapter 11

The Stigma

During family gatherings, Luke's absence was tangible, and no one dared to ask about him anymore.

I knew that people were talking about him behind my back, which made me uneasy. I put on a brave face, pretending that everything was okay. Still, there was an unspoken tension in the air regarding Luke's drug addiction. To my dismay, my cousin had told everyone in the family that Luke had stolen money from her purse during her visit to my house. She was unaware that my aunt had told me what she had said. However, my cousin had failed to mention that I had returned the money to her.

It was disheartening to witness how some people seemed to take pleasure in my struggles. Even our neighbours, with whom we used to have friendly conversations, began to distance themselves from us. Their children, who used to be friends with Luke, stopped coming around altogether.

Then I heard that Luke was hanging out at the corner shop, asking people for money or food.

I would try to avoid going there, terrified that I might bump into him. However, one day I did run into him, and it broke my heart to see him in such a state.

I asked him not to approach me when he saw me outside. The sight of Luke sleeping on the streets, looking and smelling like a tramp, was gut-wrenching. It was painful to see how much he had let himself go and how little he seemed to care about his well-being. Whenever I saw him at the shop, my heart felt as though it was being repeatedly crushed.

Zach's aunt called, expressing her fury after seeing Luke living on the street. She shared with Zach that Luke was currently staying with her. However, Zach knew this was not the solution and warned her against it, telling her that Luke might steal from them. This did not sit well with the aunt, and she responded angrily, accusing Zach of speaking ill of his son.

Despite the tension, Zach reluctantly told her not to contact him when her belongings were missing. He suggested that she call the police instead. Three days later, I received a call from Zach's aunt, informing me that Luke had stolen her jewellery and some wooden boards she kept in her backyard. I urged her to call the police, but she refused.

Unfortunately, this was the last we heard from her.

As I reflected on our family's struggles with addiction, I wondered, yet again, why this was happening to us. Immediately Mr Davids, my former high school teacher, who'd shared his own story of addiction, came to my mind. It dawned on me that addiction could affect anyone, regardless of background, race, education or social status. I began to understand that I was not to blame for Luke's addiction and that it was an illness that required treatment and support.

Chapter 12

Prison – My Nightmare

During the day, I pretended to be happy, putting on a brave face for the sake of my family. But at night, when the world was quiet and still, I cried until I fell asleep. My heart ached for Luke. And for Alisa. And for Zach. And myself.

In my free time, I frantically searched the internet for information on drugs and addiction, desperate to understand what my son was going through. I read every article I could find, watched countless documentaries, and combed through forums and support groups. I even reached out to addiction specialists and counsellors, hoping to find answers to help my son break free from its hold.

But the more I learned, the more hopeless I felt. The world of drugs, gangs and prison seemed dark and terrifying, full of danger and despair. I couldn't understand how people could willingly choose to destroy their own lives and the lives of those around them. I was sick to my stomach.

My worst fears came true when I received a call from Luke. He was at the police station, arrested for theft. I called Zach at work, but he was tied up in his Friday meeting and couldn't come immediately. I was beside myself with concern and unease.

I sent him a text message, hoping he would see it soon.

Finally, after what felt like an eternity, Zach called me back. He sounded worried and concerned when I told him about Luke's situation. He promised to come home as soon as possible, but he couldn't leave the meeting right away.

As I waited for Zach to return, my mind raced with worry and anxiety. What had happened to Luke? Why was he at the police station? My heart was racing, and I couldn't sit still.

Finally, Zach came home, and we immediately got into the car and drove to the police station. The drive stretched on endlessly, and I couldn't stop thinking about all the possible scenarios of what could have happened to Luke.

When we arrived, we spoke with one of the officers on duty, who informed us that Luke was being held on a theft charge and would appear in court on Monday and would then be taken to state prison. I felt utterly helpless. As the officer guided us down the long, dark corridor, my heart sank as we approached Luke's cell. He sat, hunched over on a small, hard bench, his head hung low in despair. The gloom of the cell enveloped him and the silence was deafening. I felt a lump form in my throat as I gazed at my son, who looked like a shadow of his former self.

We stood there for what felt like an eternity, looking at Luke as he stared down at the floor, lost in his thoughts. The air was thick with tension and sadness, and I could feel an ache within me deepening with every passing moment.

Finally, without drawing attention to our presence, we turned and walked away, leaving Luke in his dark and lonely cell. As we left the police station, I felt empty, lost and completely heartbroken. The weight of the situation was overwhelming, and I couldn't find the words to express the depth of my despair.

Days passed and turned into weeks. I became increasingly anxious, fearing the worst for Luke. I was terrified of what might happen to him in prison.

I looked up contact numbers of prisons in the telephone directory and called, but no one could find any trace of him. My social worker friend said she would assist me in uncovering what had happened to him, but even she found no trace of him.

After a month of agony, the phone finally rang. It was Luke and his hushed voice conveyed a sense of desperation. He pleaded with me to get him out of prison, saying he couldn't stand being in there with the other inmates. He promised to change and be a better person if only we would bail him out. I was conflicted, torn between wanting Luke to face the consequences of his actions and the knowledge that prison can be a dangerous place. Eventually, I persuaded Zach to pay the bail, and we went to prison to get Luke.

As we parked our car near the prison, my resolve faltered. I had promised to go in with Zach to get Luke, but now I wasn't sure if I could handle it. As Zach got out and started walking towards the imposing gates of the prison, a wave of fear washed over me. As Zach disappeared through the prison gates, I felt alone and helpless sitting in the car. The people I saw coming in and out of the entrance looked intimidating, with their gold teeth and flashy cars. This was a completely different world from what I was used to, a world where danger lurked.

As the minutes ticked by, I felt increasingly anxious. Whenever someone walked past the car, I tensed up, expecting the worst. I knew I had to pull myself together, but I couldn't shake off the feeling of impending doom.

Finally, after what felt like an eternity, Zach emerged from the prison gates with Luke in tow. I let out a sigh of relief. Luke was safe, and he was coming home.

He looked different somehow, older and more worn down by his time in prison. He thanked us both and promised to change. But that promise was hard to believe. I couldn't shake the feeling that Luke was still the same person who had committed the crime and ended up in prison.

That evening, we talked about the documentaries on prison life I had watched and how they frightened me. To my surprise, Luke told me he had watched them too.

Addiction is a powerful force, and it wasn't long before he succumbed to his old habits and disappeared. Eventually, we received a call from him saying he was at the police station.

Despite his plea for help, we decided to disregard his call. After three months had passed, Luke appeared on our doorstep, claiming he had been released from prison. I, however, was not in the mood to listen to his story.

Overwhelmed by everything that had transpired, I asked him to leave.

The gravity of the situation had taken its toll, and I felt sickened by it all. The weight was too much to bear.

Chapter 13

The Healer

During one of Abu's classes, a woman shared a unique treatment method she received for her constant migraines and neck pain. She explained the technique, and I felt drawn to the approach. Intrigued by what she said, I asked for more details about this unconventional healer. She gave me the woman's phone number.

Joanne answered when I called the number. Her sweet and gentle voice calmed me. I made an appointment to see her.

At the appointment, Joanne began with a foot massage and then asked me to lie down on the therapy bed. She assessed my chakras and energy field, which are not visible to the human eye but can be captured by specialised cameras. Although I didn't fully understand what she was saying, I trusted her and allowed her to place her hands on me, slowly moving them from my head to my feet. She spoke in a soft, hypnotic voice, revealing that a childhood event still affected me. She suggested that my lack of trust contributed to the anxiety attacks and hypertension.

Joanne then asked if I felt any physical pain, and I told her about the ache in my heart. She explained that this energy was not solely mine but a part of my family's past generations. Although this revelation surprised me, I felt relieved that someone understood what I was experiencing. 'Did your mother also suffer from hypertension?' Joanne asked, noticing my nod in response. She guided me in her warm and soothing voice, 'I'm going to take you back in time to see where it all began. Please close your eyes and remember that you are safe here. You can open your eyes at any time.' As she began to count from one to ten, I felt increasingly relaxed until I was entirely at ease when she reached ten.

From a distance, Joanne prompted me to describe the ache in my heart. I explained the feeling in detail, and she asked if I could remember feeling this way when I was eighteen. After a moment's reflection, I shook my head in response. Although I could see myself at eighteen, there was no heartache present.

'Let's travel even further back to when you were about sixteen,' Joanne suggested.

But still, I could not recall any pain.

Joanne continued to work with me through younger ages. Her soothing voice and gentle touch gave me a sense of safety and trust, allowing me to let go of my anxiety and tension.

'Stay with the pain,' Joanne's voice remained gentle as we delved into my past experiences. 'Let's return to when you were about three or younger.'

With my eyes closed, I concentrated on Joanne's words.

Suddenly, I saw myself as a little girl standing at my aunt's place. My heart pounded, and tears flowed down my cheeks. 'I'm three years old,' I said, struggling to keep my voice steady. 'I'm scared. We're at my aunt's place. My father is drunk, and he's fighting with Mom. His angry, loud voice makes me and my siblings afraid of him. He always frightened me as a child.'

Joanne listened attentively to me sharing with her the incident of that day, and after a while, she asked, 'Do you want to say anything to your mom?'

I felt a lump in my throat and hesitated. 'I can't. I don't have a voice. I couldn't speak to my parents or any adult as a child,' I said.

Joanne encouraged me, 'You have a voice now. What would you like to say to her?'

I took a deep breath and looked at my mother. Tears streamed down my face as I asked her, 'Why did Mummy endure him for so long? Could Mummy not see how Dad was destroying you, destroying all of us?' I broke down and sobbed uncontrollably.

Joanne comforted me until I was drained. 'Is there anything else you'd like to ask your mother?' she asked gently.

I shook my head. 'No.'

Joanne inquired about my mother's response, and I struggled to compose myself before responding, 'She's looking at me, and she's apologising. She thought that what she did was best for the family.'

After a moment, Joanne directed my attention to my father and asked, 'Do you have anything to say to or ask him?'

I nodded and, as I imagined myself as the little three-year-old girl, I felt my jaw clench and my teeth grind together. Finally, I asked my father, 'Why were you so terrible to Mummy and to all of us?'

He didn't answer. Instead, he gazed at me with the saddest eyes and I felt a knot form in my throat. The air felt thick and suffocating and I struggled to breathe. I gasped for air and tried to hold back my sobs, but eventually I broke down and tears streamed down my face.

Joanne stood by me, offering me comfort and support as I cried. We worked through the pain together, and I felt a sense of release and healing.

Joanne spoke softly, 'Take the hand of little Ella and let her sit next to you.'

As I imagined doing so, I felt a wave of joy at the thought of holding her warm, soft little body close to mine.

'Now, ask her how she feels. Listen to whatever she is saying,' Joanne instructed.

'She says that she's sad and hurt,' I replied.

Joanne urged me to apologise to little Ella for her sadness and to wipe away her tears. I was to reassure her that everything would be alright and that I would take care of her. I spoke to little Ella until I saw a sweet smile on her face. Joanne then advised me to hold little Ella close to my body and to let her body slowly merge with mine. She asked me to feel her presence in my heart, where little Ella would always be kept safe and protected, where no one could harm her. I could shower her with love and protect her whenever desired, and she would remain with me always. I basked in the feeling of love for that little child within me. 'When you are ready, you may open your eyes,' Joanne said softly.

It took me a few minutes to open my eyes. I felt a huge weight lifted off me, and I was in awe and grateful for having met this remarkable woman.

As I was about to depart, Joanne imparted some valuable advice. 'Sometimes, the challenges you face are not yours alone. They may have been inherited from your parents, grandparents or earlier ancestors. However, you have the power to put an end to it.'

Her words infused me with energy and determination to face any obstacle that came my way. Before leaving, I promptly made an appointment for the following week. I walked out feeling lighter and more at peace with myself.

Chapter 14

The Intervention

It was a cold winter evening with heavy rains. Luke had been living on the streets for three months and seemed to have lost his way. That's when we were greeted by a strange woman, Zilina, outside our door. She introduced herself and asked if she could come in and talk to us about Luke.

Initially, I was hesitant and looked at her with wary eyes, but she seemed friendly and concerned. So, I invited her in and I asked her to sit down in the lounge while I called Zach. Zilina started by telling us that she lived two blocks from our house and had met Luke through her son. He had been sleeping at her place for two days, and she had come to us because Luke had told her he was not allowed to go home.

Zilina said that Luke had been on drugs but had stopped and was now waiting outside. She asked if we could give him a chance and let him come in and speak to us. Reluctantly, we agreed, amidst the howling winds and pouring rain outside. Zilina went to the door to call Luke.

Luke appeared at our doorstep, head down, soaking wet and looking like a mess while the rain poured down even harder. I rose from my seat and gently shut the door behind Luke as he entered, returning to Zach's side and sitting next to him again.

My heart sank as I looked at our son and saw addiction's toll on his body.

'So, what is your story now?' I asked anxiously, feeling anger and heartbreak too.

'Mom... Dad. I want to ask you if I can come home. I don't want to live like this anymore,' he said, his head still bent.

'You know you can't live here anymore. It pains me to say this, but looking at you makes me feel uncomfortable and uneasy,' I replied. My frustration and mistrust intensified as I spoke, and I could feel my stomach churning with anxiety. I inquired if he was prepared to assume accountability for his wrongdoings, hoping that he was willing to take responsibility for his actions. 'Yes, Mom,' he replied quietly.

Without saying a word to Luke, Zach got on his phone and called our neighbour, Captain Adam. While he was on the call, I decided to call Bradley, who had previously helped Luke with his addiction recovery. Bradley was unable to come because he had a personal emergency to attend to. I explained our situation to him, and he suggested that the best course of action would be to take Luke to the police station and then promptly admit him to a rehabilitation centre. He promised to help us find a rehab for Luke.

About fifteen minutes passed before Captain Adam arrived. As he approached Luke, disappointment was written all over his face. Captain Adam had known Luke since childhood and had watched him grow up in the community. The sight of Luke in this state seemed to dishearten him. Despite this, he addressed Luke with a sense of urgency and firmness, determined to make him see the gravity of his actions.

'Your father told me you said you want to change,' he began.

Luke responded with a meek, 'Yes, Mr Adam,' his head still down.

Captain Adam continued earnestly. 'I have seen you growing up here and playing with my son. Look what you've done to yourself and your family. Do you realise all the suffering you caused your family?'

Now attentive, Luke responded, 'Yes, Mr Adam, I know... but I want to change. I am sorry.' His words were laced with remorse.

The captain recommended that Zach and Luke go to the police station the following day. He assured us that, even if there were a case against Luke, the police wouldn't detain him if we could demonstrate that he was willing to enter rehab immediately. Captain Adam then addressed Luke directly, expressing his hope that he would make positive changes to his life.

As the conversation with Captain Adam ended, my mind was already racing with questions and concerns. One question, in particular, was at the forefront of my mind: where would Luke sleep tonight? I couldn't bear the thought of him sleeping outside in the cold, but I also couldn't trust him enough to let him sleep inside our home.

Feeling uneasy and confused, I expressed my concern.

Zilina offered to let Luke sleep at her place for another night. I expressed concern that he might steal from her. Zilina was optimistic and reassured me that she would call the police if anything should happen.

Zach turned to Luke and instructed him to come to our house the next morning at eight so that he could take him to the police station.

The next day, while Zach and Luke were out, Alisa approached me. She said she had overheard everything of the previous evening and had decided to move out. She had already made plans to stay with a friend.

No matter how much I tried to convince her to stay and talk to me, she seemed determined to leave. She expressed that she felt our whole world revolved around Luke and nobody cared about her.

I was shocked and felt like I had failed her as a parent.

As I watched her pack her things, I was crushed. I didn't know how to fix things or make them better for Alisa. All I could do was tell her I loved her and didn't want to lose her.

It felt like the ground was opening beneath me as I watched her leave.

Chapter 15

The Pearl – Rehabilitation Centre

The following day at precisely eight o'clock, Luke arrived at our doorstep, ready to be accompanied by his father to the police station.

They explained the purpose of their visit to the officer on duty. The officer could not locate any information about Luke in his computer system. However, when Luke provided a false name that he had previously used, the officer discovered that he had been charged with theft.

Zach informed him that Luke was a drug addict and would be entering a rehab facility that day.

The officer provided them with the date Luke was scheduled to appear in court to face criminal theft charges.

Zach located a rehab facility on a farm willing to take Luke in.

I was feeling an array of emotions, including anger and exhaustion. I needed some space to process everything that had happened.

Over the next few weeks, Zach remained in contact with the rehab. Six weeks later, we received an invitation from them to attend a family meeting.

As I sat in the family meeting at the fourth rehab centre, I felt utterly exhausted. When it was my turn to speak, I mustered the courage to share my thoughts. 'I am just so tired,' I said, my voice shaking with emotion. 'I feel completely drained. I don't even know why I came here today. Addiction is Luke's struggle, not mine. He's the addict, not me. I don't want to be a part of this "drug dance" anymore,' I said to the group. 'It's time for me to focus on my own needs and well-being. If Zach chooses to continue being involved, that's up to him, but I need to step back.'

As I spoke those words, I took a slow deep breath, feeling the fresh country air energising my body, and then exhaled a sigh of relief. It was as if a weight had been lifted from my chest and shoulders. I had carried so much guilt and shame for so long, feeling like it was my responsibility to handle everyone else's problems. But now, finally, I was letting it all go.

At the same time, though, I also felt a deep sense of sadness. It was hard to admit that I couldn't fix everything for everyone else. I had to let go and trust that Luke would find his path, even if it meant going in a different direction than me.

As I looked around the room during the family meeting, I could tell that some parents were new to this experience. They seemed shocked when the counsellor said, 'Rehabilitation is not a magic wand, and recovery is a process. It won't happen overnight.' I remembered the first time I heard those words, it was like a gut punch, a sudden realisation that it could be a long and challenging journey.

I had been hoping for a quick fix, a way to make everything better instantly.

I felt a sense of sadness and grief. This was not how I had imagined my life would be.

I had always been a planner, a doer, someone who could make things happen, and I was lost.

I had dealt with addiction in my family for almost eight years by then, and I knew first-hand that recovery was a journey, not a quick fix.

During the meeting, though, I had a revelation. The counsellor said something that resonated with me: we should not view a relapse as a failure but rather as a lesson. This was a powerful reminder that recovery is not a linear process. There could be setbacks and challenges along the way. Still, each could be an opportunity to create more awareness and change the approach to recovery.

The counsellor also emphasised the importance of family support in the addict's recovery process.

After the family meeting, we gathered for tea, and that's when I met Papa, the father of the counsellor. Only then did I discover that the rehab centre was a family-run business. As we talked, Papa introduced me to his wife, the matriarch of all the boys at the centre. They welcomed us and we felt part of their family. Their warmth and caring was evident. It felt like we were part of a close-knit community rather than just another group of visitors.

During our conversation, Papa said something that profoundly impacted on me. He said, 'You must always remember that you are never too good to be bad, and you are never too bad to be good.' Although I heard it many times before, these words resonated deeply that day, and I realised they held a profound truth. No one is immune to making mistakes and everyone can be redeemed. Embracing this reality with humility and grace was crucial for me. His words made me feel hopeful, reminding me there is always a way forward.

As the days passed, Luke's commitment to recovery became evident. He actively participated in the therapy and support group sessions. He was putting in the hard work, and we could see the positive changes in his behaviour and attitude. Seeing him slowly but surely rebuilding his life, one step at a time, was a joy. His progress was visible and measurable.

He took responsibility for his actions, and we could sense the determination in his voice and the hope in his eyes. As a family, we continued to support Luke, visiting him regularly and offering encouragement.

We were cautiously optimistic that, this time, he had turned a corner in his journey to recovery.

Chapter 16

The Social Worker

In addition to the rehab programme, the families of the recovering addicts were encouraged to make an appointment with the in-house social worker, Rose. She had made a strong impression on me with her thoughtful and informative talk at the previous family meeting, so Zach and I decided to make an appointment to see her.

As we sat down with Rose, she asked us how things were going with Luke. We shared with her that he seemed to be progressing well. His dedication to attending therapy, support group sessions, and helping out at the rehab impressed us.

Rose asked us a vital question, 'What would you do if Luke returned to drugs?'

It was a question I had been grappling with for a long time; one that filled me with uncertainty and fear. But after much reflection and soul-searching, I had come to a decision. 'I gave this much thought after our last meeting here, Rose,' I said. 'It is time for me to let go. Luke is now twenty-two years old. Although I know it might take time for him to get back on his feet, I realise he is an adult and needs to take responsibility for his actions. I am done with enabling.'

I felt a sense of relief. It was not easy, but I knew it was the right decision for me. I knew that if I continued to focus on Luke's addiction and neglected my own well-being, I would not be able to continue living in a healthy and fulfilling way.

After carefully reflecting on the situation, I had come to the realisation that Luke had an abundance of resources and support systems available to him, such as the caring individuals at the rehab centre, his therapy and support group sessions, and people like Rose, who genuinely wanted to see him succeed.

I acknowledged that, while I loved and cared about Luke deeply, I could not bear the burden of his recovery; nor should I.

It was clear that Luke needed to take responsibility for his healing and consciously choose a life of sobriety. By staying on the path of recovery, he would have access to an incredible network of people and resources dedicated to helping him every step of the way.

And so, I let go of the idea that I could fix everything for Luke.

As Rose turned her attention to Zach, I listened with interest to hear what he had to say.

'We have discussed this,' he replied to Rose's question about his feelings. 'We will support him in recovery but not addiction.' His words were resolute and firm, and I felt proud of him for standing by his principles.

Rose nodded in agreement. 'That's great. I'm glad you came to that conclusion,' she said. 'You can't change Luke or make choices for him. He needs to make his own choices.' Her tone was matter of fact, and I knew that she was right.

Despite my desire to control Luke's life and shield him from harm, I recognised that he was an adult who needed to take accountability for his choices.

As I recounted to Rose what I had said to Luke, I felt a surge of bravery and determination. 'I told him that he can no longer live with us. He can visit, but he needs to work for what he wants. With this opportunity he has been given to be here at the rehab centre, he can turn his life around if he puts in the effort. I know he has the intelligence to accomplish anything he sets his mind to. He needs to use it to his advantage.'

'Coming from a family with a history of addiction, do you realise you have the power to break the cycle of addiction, Ella?' Rose asked me. 'If you break it now, it will play a huge role in preventing addiction from continuing to your future generations.'

Her words hit me like a thunderbolt. I had never thought of it in that way before.

Suddenly, I felt a sense of purpose and responsibility. I could make a difference in my family's future, which was a powerful motivation to stay strong and committed to my decision.

Rose directed her attention to Zach and emphasised the importance of fostering a positive relationship with Luke. 'He needs you,' she expressed. 'Did you know he considers you as his role model? Just be mindful not to enable him,' she warned.

I observed Zach nodding in agreement, and I sensed that we were both on the same page. I felt a new-found hope as we departed from Rose's office.

I took comfort in the fact that we had the backing of people like Rose and the rehabilitation centre. Their aid and advice assured me that we could overcome the obstacles ahead and come out stronger and more resilient than ever.

Chapter 17

The Marriage Counsellor

As Luke's addiction recovery progressed at the rehab centre, I noticed that my marriage with Zach was slowly crumbling. Our ability to communicate had disappeared, and it felt like we had nothing in common beyond our children. Being preoccupied with Luke, I had failed to see the extent to which our relationship had eroded.

All my attempts to fix things with Zach had been unsuccessful, and it was time to seek outside support. So, I suggested that we see a marriage counsellor to get professional help to repair the damage that had been done to our relationship.

Zach's constant work commitments made it seem like he had no time for anything else. He often brought work home, leaving me feeling neglected and feeling as if he were avoiding me. It felt like I was the only one trying to keep our relationship afloat, and I knew that I couldn't continue doing it alone.

I arranged to see a skilled psychologist named Sharon and travelled to her office with Zach to attend our appointment. She greeted us with a warm smile and cordially invited us in. She began the session by asking us a few questions, such as the reason for our visit and who had initiated the meeting.

In response, I explained that I had learned about her through a friend's recommendation and had subsequently arranged for Zach to accompany me to the session. I opened up to Sharon and shared some of the challenges we faced in our marriage, such as communication breakdowns and emotional distance. I also provided a brief overview of our history with addiction, which impacted our relationship in various ways. I gave her a brief overview of how our son's drug addiction had become the primary focus of our lives. I expressed that, now that Luke was on his journey to recovery, the underlying issues in our marriage had become even more apparent. I admitted that our communication had utterly broken down and I had grown weary of trying to engage with Zach.

In that moment, feeling completely hopeless, I earnestly requested Sharon's professional assistance in saving our marriage.

Sharon's focus then turned to Zach, and she asked him to share his perspective on why he had agreed to come to the appointment. He initially attempted to lighten the mood with a joke, suggesting that I had dragged him along. However, he quickly became serious when he saw the sincerity in Sharon's unwavering gaze. He candidly admitted that I had been urging him to communicate more. Still, he felt unsure about what I wanted to hear or how to express his feelings. He thought he was doing his best to provide for our family but didn't know what else he could do.

As the hour-long session progressed, Sharon led us through some exercises and discussions to help us better understand our perspectives and identify the issues in our marriage. She then assigned an activity to complete as homework, which served as a wake-up call for both of us. It made me recognise how much had broken down in our relationship and family and how much effort would be needed to rebuild our connection. Despite the challenging work ahead, I felt committed to doing whatever it took to save our relationship and keep our family together.

Chapter 18

Alisa, Daughter of Moon

The impact of Luke's drug abuse, dishonesty and theft on Alisa, was immense. As a child, Alisa was reserved and content with her own company.

Since she was introspective, she chose to spend time alone. She did not care for the latest fashions and fads that others her age obsessed over.

Alisa was oblivious to the devastating effects of drug use. She was simply not interested.

As she grew older, Alisa craved independence. She started making money by selling goods at the local market. With this new-found freedom she bought things she loved.

Luke began stealing her things. Alisa discussed the missing items and the suspect with me several times, but even after I had spoken to Luke, he continued on this destructive path. I was lost. I had betrayed my own daughter. I did not know how to protect her. I did not know how to remedy the situation.

She felt trapped in her home. She was uncomfortable inviting friends over. She feared what her brother might get up to.

At other times, Alisa felt she had to act as her brother's guardian. She watched his every move and accompanied him to the city and the market compelled to keep an eye on him.

Our family looked forward to going on holiday to discover and experience new places, and since Luke's destructive behaviour, the holiday became more of an escape from the constant turmoil at home.

However, trouble followed us wherever we went. It was as if we were cursed and weren't allowed to take a break from the chaos that overwhelmed our days. We couldn't escape our problems no matter how far we travelled.

Alisa would take a friend along and it felt good to see her happy.

But whatever the cause, it always seemed to end sadly, if not badly. The feeling of hopelessness that things would never improve was all-pervading.

Our return home from vacation was consistently met with more bad news about Luke. It was devastating that things had not improved in our absence. Yet, despite the disappointment and heartache, the holiday was a relief from the madness of our everyday lives. It was a chance to recharge, to escape the constant stress and anxiety, and to remind ourselves that there was still beauty and joy in the world.

For a short while, both Alisa and Luke worked together at the local market. It was there that Alisa noticed that her brother couldn't function unless he had taken drugs. It disturbed her, and she tried to distance herself from him. One fateful day, a city officer came upon Luke, heavily drugged while at work. Alisa witnessed how the city officer escorted him from the building.

The news of his arrest reached our household And we were summoned to the city buildings, where the severity of Luke's drug use was made clear..

Alisa felt ashamed and embarrassed at work, and no longer wanted to associate with her brother.

After that, Luke's addiction spiralled out of control and it wasn't long before his actions caught up with him.

He was caught stealing, and the law sent him to jail.

The news of his arrest was a heavy blow because we constantly hoped that, miraculously, Luke would turn his life around. Our hopes and dreams for his future were shattered, and we were left to pick up the pieces of our broken family. The sense of loss and sadness weighed heavily as we struggled to come to terms with reality.

After three months, Luke was released, but Alisa couldn't bring herself to see him. The fear and disappointment of what he had become were too much. And when she finally did see him, she pretended not to recognise him, because she didn't want to face, again, the reality of what he had done to himself and our family.

Alisa saw me expelling Luke from our family home several times. However, each time he managed to find his way back in. Alisa was disgusted by his ragged and unkempt reappearances from living on the dangerous streets of Wasteland.

But no matter how many times I promised to keep him out, my heart would soften when I saw him in such a desperate state. I would give in to my sympathy and allow him to return, even though I knew it would cause further turmoil and heartache.

The cycle of rejection and forgiveness was never-ending, causing much stress and confusion for our family. And so, for Alisa, it wasn't easy to sleep in peace. She would sleep lightly, fearing something might happen to her, or to me or Zach. She double-checked locks at night and locked her bedroom door.

Alisa had developed an intense hostility towards our family, and especially her brother. One day, in anger, Alisa lunged towards her brother, pressing him against the wall in a stranglehold and glared at him with contempt. Overwhelmed by her emotions and actions, she released him and collapsed in tears.

She saw me hide away the family's valuables and lock the doors during the day. She saw me hide our book collections in the ceiling, thinking that Luke would not find them there. He found them all, and sold them again, for cash, at the bookseller.

One day I went to the bookseller and found thirty-three of our books there. Some had descended through generations, now gone to finance the vapours of the poison.

Alisa reached a point where she felt lost and uncertain about her life and she questioned the meaning and purpose of her existence, and yearned for a sense of direction. More than anything, she longed to feel loved and validated as she struggled to find a sense of belonging in our family.

She felt isolated and alone amidst the chaos and she craved a way out of the madness. Eventually, she found comfort in a relationship that gave her a glimpse of the happiness she wanted.

Her desire to escape the endless reminders of our family's struggles led her to leave home. In doing so, she hoped to distance herself from the disease that had plagued us.

With the promise of a happier life away from home, Alisa chose to cut off contact with me and Zach. It was a difficult decision, but she believed it was necessary for her well-being and happiness.

During the first year of her new-found independence, Alisa enjoyed the freedom of not dealing with the drama and chaos in our family. She explored her interests, met new people and experienced life on her terms. However, as the second year approached, Alisa realised how much she had left behind and missed us. She found it hard to accept that her life would never be the same as before, and the gravity of her situation was burdensome to her.

She had felt like an outsider, and our family's history with the disease intensified her sense of alienation. Her struggle to articulate her feelings only aggravated her troubles, and she feared revealing too much about herself.

This fear only heightened her sense of detachment, causing her to retreat deeper into herself.

After Alisa left home, Luke went to rehab. Over time, Luke began to make progress in his rehabilitation, and Alisa would visit him with Zach and me at the rehabilitation centre. These visits provided a rare opportunity for our family to spend time together and reconnect. We would sometimes spend the afternoon catching up and reminiscing about the better old times.

Despite the terrifying journey we had been on, we found moments of joy and togetherness.

As time went by, Luke gradually started taking control of his life, secured employment at the rehab centre, and after a few years, got married.

And so, from Alisa's perspective,the siblings never had a sister and brother relationship, and she could not picture that they ever would.

Luke would occasionally visit Alisa, but she, fearing what he might want and take from her, had nothing to offer – no connection, no conversation. He would often leave after only a few minutes.

Eventually she realised he was probably trying to build bridges and make a start to mending their relationship. As courageous as she was, as appreciative as she may cautiously feel, she was still too afraid, too fragile. What might become of her if her mind and soul were broken too? She felt her heart sing in woeful, sometimes angry, sometimes painful, sorrow.

She felt that addiction had destroyed any family relatedness she may have had with Zach and me, and so what remained had fragmented and drifted apart, along with her self-esteem and self-worth.

Her fear had gripped her so tightly that she couldn't bring herself to speak to anyone.

Like a leaf trembling in a fierce wind, she felt powerless against the forces that threatened to overwhelm her.

Gradually, over time, Alisa's relationship with me improved. We were able to share and laugh and, when not together, we exchanged long letters in streams by constant messengers.

She and her father had started to speak, although in short conversations.

Once he came to her during the day and he worked on his books at her side, for such pleasant company was a comfort to a lonesome father. Behind his mask, he concealed those hits he had endured since the poison arrived that day. They spoke about their work, and he had lunch with her in a quiet corner. It felt awkward to Alisa, after the darkness and harsh words. She realised afterwards that it was probably a steppingstone toward better days ahead.

Alisa told me that she loved and missed us – her mother and her father – and felt as if time in her childhood and young adult life had been stolen by that thief, addiction, and turned into a disease.

Alisa was glad Luke was not abusing drugs anymore.

Glad that he made that decision.

She doubted that she would ever have a deep bond with him, for she protected her heart lest he broke it again.

While she yearned for his reintegration into our family unit, she was nonetheless affected by the years of sorrow that had left her fearful of letting him in.

Chapter 19

Mom in the Mirror

Incredible anger; that was how I felt as I stared at my reflection in the mirror.

My best friend Lily had to teach me how to breathe from a brown paper bag.

I was sitting cross-legged on the stone floor while Lily tried to calm me as if holding my wild horses. My life had become unstable.

I did not know of those evil forces.

I was the enabler in this business of darkness, according to Lily.

I was tired. I was exhausted. I was drained.

And it repeated and repeated, and it wouldn't go away, and I didn't even know how I got there.

We lived on the Bay of Falsehood.

Like a house of cards, our family started falling apart. As if our picture framed a crack, my marriage was on the rocks, my life about to shatter, all by the sands of those sad times of grief and constant sorrow.

All I knew was that it started when I found Luke doing drugs.

I told Lily I was grateful for her help.

She shrugged and said, 'You know, Ella, it's all very well you saying that, kind and all, but I'd prefer, if you wouldn't mind, putting that in an affidavit.' Then she smiled and went back to her crocheting.

Our house was no longer a home. Our house felt like a prison. It was like a chameleon morphing into a mental hospital where we constantly fought. I had contemplated separating from my husband, for I was at war and fighting with almost everyone.

The disease brought changes to my life. Before this dark force, it had felt like the seasons of my life flowed seamlessly and beautifully from one to another in a fixed regularity. Our family was what society termed successful.

But quickly the regular patterns of success were lost and life became uncivilised.

'You must learn about birds like Aristophanes and find the missing radical,' said Lily. 'Part of the reason people like us get into trouble is that we only know half of the story.'

Now, this is what I'm getting at, and this is the type of stuff that I had to deal with, and what follows is exactly how I dealt with it.

'Go to hell, Lily Bright!' and then I stormed off. Addiction, a new cunning force had infiltrated our lives, threatening to overshadow the familiar rhythms of our regular seasons. It was a force to be reckoned with, one that demanded attention and respect, yet it was foreign and the undoing of me.

Addiction arrived on our doorstep like the onset of a cold, dark winter causing mix-ups, mess-ups and unpredictable timing and left me without a plan. And I always had a plan. Lily began to frame a new way for the seasons of my mind. Yet I was determined to try and follow those same old seasons and the same old ways, and I did not realise they were all gone.

Lily was unpacking my life with great organisation. So I let her be.

I was no longer the master of my universe and no longer reacting appropriately.

The instinctive actions of a mom who'd carried a child nine months below her heart did not apply to these new seasons of times of sacrifice.

I partly blamed my husband, Zach, for our son's addiction because I was in denial.

My practice of mothering was unsuitable to confront addiction, and all that I did was wholly inappropriate. So, I blamed Zach. I felt Zach wasn't there to support our son against addiction.

Addiction!

I felt Zach wasn't there when Luke needed Zach's nurturing and nourishing and the necessary cultivation that had been missing, supposing our son was the apple tree in our garden. In that case, we must have better tended to it by the elements of nature – sun and moon, wind and rain – so that we might have regulated the quality and quantity of growth.

Zach and I continued not directing with encouragement and inspiration but with fear. Our branches to higher understanding had been cut off long ago.

Yet, instinctively I knew of the changing of seasons and the mounting winds.

And the keys?

The keys kept the doors locked, and I paced around the house with the keys hidden by the leather belt I wore as if a reminder to the young man I'd brought into this world of the authority I held as a parent. As if leather might stop him from going through closed doors.

And if they could, those doors would've served as encouragement to a greater purpose and a message of hope for all humanity and not a product of strategic planning that I failed to perceive in my fury.

The doors were locked and I was afraid to open the doors of humiliation, shame and sorrow.

My forefathers were bound in chains, taken aboard ships and forced into slavery, as if they were mere cargo carried by the winds of misfortune. Maybe that is why I'm perplexed about the origins of my broken and damaged life.

And that was the disease.

A few days later, I was on the deck again with Lily. She was knitting as we talked. Lily only knits on weekends, so it must have been a Saturday or Sunday.

We sat together quietly. I was looking over the Bay of Falsehood.

Lily spoke. 'You know, I think I must have been Alexander the Great's sister in a past life, only much smarter and more ambitious than him.'

Now that was a lot for me to take in at that point. And then I started to think that Lily Bright was also on drugs, and I did not know that she was to be the medicine for this disease.

And so, I carried the keys in my leather sling bag, which I could beat as a drum wherever I marched around the house like a manufactured deranged Goliath to David's secret chords. I kept the doors locked at all times, afraid Luke would steal our money and our jewellery as he had before.

From an endless list, he also pocketed the watch of my great grandfather.

Luke stole all our things to support his drug habit. I would sit down with him for hours, trying to speak some sense into him and reason with him. At other times I would lose my nerve and vent my anger at him. I hoped he would understand and see how his drug abuse affected our family. I cleaned up after him. I washed his clothes. We bought him clothes and gifts only to find out later that he had sold them in a trade for poison.

Then, Zach bought him a guitar. He sold his guitar after a few weeks, and then again, the liar.

Yet in this dark business, it turned out that I am one of the suspects.

That is, according to Lily.

Lily Bright is my best friend. Something I'm telling you for a second time, for it's as if there is a duality between Lily and her secret organisation.

Lily was an unconventional woman with a detached perspective who taught arts from her bungalow. She had a talent for rhyming and manipulating sounds in her teachings. Earlier that day, Lily experienced a turning point that marked the beginning of a new chapter in her life, filled with both joy and pain. Lily recounted a tale to me about powerful individuals in positions of authority who display no hesitation in taking human lives. These individuals had embraced corruption and rock music as part of their agenda.

To accomplish this, they manipulated people's addictions and used music to recruit followers.

An example of this was the rise of rap music, which had created a generation of radicals drawn to its aggressive lyrics, rebellious spirit and trouble. Slang, such as 'a chicken', which refers to a kilogram of cocaine and 'flippin' chickens', which means selling drugs for a higher price than its purchased price, were common words used to attract younger listeners. By exploiting addiction and utilising music as a tool, these individuals found benefits in their actions.

This rap, rock and drugs were the business Luke got mixed up in and thereby penned in.

Yet Lily wanted the changes.

Lily's hand felt warm if you held it, for she was sincere and friendly.

In spring and summer, Lily sacrificed herself to her industry of beauty, health and perfection of life and the out-of-season, especially weekdays, for the whisper she'd left for the country.

And so Lily Bright was on her way, saddled up and set for the plains of universal suffrage. Hair, too, cut and set; on the way to *smoke the smoke*[4].

The courtroom in the Valley of Wasteland was crowded and its appearance was almost identical to the temples in the same region. It had the same furnishing, pews, solemn arrangement, fancy dress, and pulpits for speeches. Both institutions manipulated time and divided people, with perceptions of a better social order for those participating.

Both temple and courtroom had figures of great power and influence, some of whom operated in the shadows and behind the scenes. Through the power of written or spoken words, they guided and directed people like birds soaring

4 Slang – has a dual meaning. a. to deceive, or in this context, b. battle deception

through the air and riding the winds towards their intended destination.

No sound.

Then, by wisdom and knowledge, the court handled the cases. There were intervals and spaces between 'if…,' and 'those who…', and 'which was that?'

The presentation was delivered with a high standard of quality and tone, reminiscent of the serene atmosphere of a peaceful Sunday. Power was at work with the forces of engineering, for some people liked regulation.

And so, they concocted a clever recipe of how to work what works the system.

For such are the acts of this song.

And so, Luke had to sit for ninety days, and *Tony*[5], Lily's sound engineer, on another day, would have him out in forty-five.

It was as if Lily Bright was moonlight in human form, which is why I liked her and Tony. Tony was a radical. He set the rhymes and cut the sounds. He could also borrow the master, known as *Salty*[6]. And so the people of the Valley of Wasteland got less from this warrior genius.

As a result, the use of slang had created obstacles in pursuing justice, which made it challenging for those in the Valley of Wasteland to communicate effectively. And that's why there were difficulties to court. The evolution from *rap to wrap*[7] occurred because wrap words flow smoothly and effortlessly from the mouth.

---

5 Tony means sophisticated and elegant manner

6 Salty means loyalty, value. pureness, truthful…

7 The change from "rap" to "wrap" is a progression from aggressive and troublesome lyrics towards a more refined and sophisticated form of verbal communication.

And Tony did this to defend and protect Lily and Luke so Lily could continue practicing yoga near her cottage, which also served as a sanctuary and a measurement for the future of well-being.

He found Lily to be an unorthodox east-side girl and worker of handicrafts to which he paid respect.

So, Lily made arrangements for Luke to be released and let in at the door.

Thus began his process of becoming a made person within the organisation to cut off the evil characters of Wasteland, who certainly did not know about this private school; nor did they know the requirements and therefore knew not to inquire.

There is a knot[8] that bound the people in the Valley of Wasteland, keeping them united and small. Such is the knowledge to those who indeed comprehend. The knot has a will and is, in fact, an enemy of the people and full of missing and most wanted radicals; their Gordian knot[9].

The missing sound is the drops of sorrow from either Salty or Lily, or both. Yet the older and more experienced in the Valley of Wasteland know of this upright situation, yet fail to connect the product of Lily Bright and Salty.

Wasteland Valley is a dangerous place with traps, deceptions, criminals and almost everything wrong with this world. Those in power manipulate the political and legal systems for personal gain, shamelessly and unscrupulously. by creating weaknesses for others and then shaming and humiliating those unaware. In response the chorus – in this

---

8 The knot bound people according to the status, class, culture, education, etc..

9 Gordian knot – metaphor for an extremely difficult problem

instance, the general public – steps forward methodically and unconsciously, supports such authors of darkened and poisoned society.

Yet, these things are not material for polite conversation.

And 'Go to hell, Lily Bright!' was just the result of words spoken in the past.

Chapter 20

The Shift

I experienced a significant shift in my approach towards life. Rather than trying to impose my desires on others or enabling them, I began to focus on myself, taking full responsibility for my actions and respecting others' choices even if they were different to mine.

This shift led to healthier relationships with those I love and choose to spend my time with.

As a parent, it was a lengthy process to understand enabling. At first, it appears to be the right thing to do, to protect your child. However, I eventually realised that by shielding him from the consequences of his actions I was depriving him of the chance to take accountability for his life.

This realisation led me to establish boundaries, learning to say no and honouring my commitments.

During this process, I learned that many things are beyond our control or influence: like our past and other's choices.

However, I also learned that, no matter what life presents us, we are free to choose how we respond. It is in this choice that our true power resides.

By recognising this power of choice, we can take control of our lives and make decisions that align with our values and goals, allowing us to live a fulfilling and meaningful life.

I started doing things that I enjoyed and was grateful to have my family back together. I was motivated to continue growing and uncovering the many layers of myself.

One of the most significant realisations during this process was that I could not change Luke or anyone else. I could only change myself. This understanding freed me from the burden of trying to control others. It allowed me to focus on my growth and development.

Overall, my journey towards understanding enabling and codependency was challenging and sometimes devastating but I gained much. It allowed me to cultivate healthier relationships, take control of my life, and to find greater fulfilment and meaning.

Chapter 21

To the Light Bridge

I found the means to reform my life before permanent damage could set in and that period and process was still a living hell.

Everyone in addiction; whether the addict, enablers or codependents, must pass through that hell as it is often a necessary step towards recovery.

However, you must know that the justice of society is not really there to help you.

You're on your own.

There is no real leadership in addiction reform.

Society is also both the enabler and the codependent in the industry of addiction.

The family in society is the sideshow in this industry. They are the topic for gossip in the community by those who trade such stories on the grapevine and point fingers.

I found justice in my heart for myself, but I also know that society is not unjust and so I became interested in social reform in this business so that I might use my experiences to help others in the same plight – and that became the next part of my journey. That became like the very beginning of a new spring.

I recovered my creative energy and began to make positive advances and those advances gave me more optimism and I became more realistic.

I know now that decline is a natural part of life. I know that ultimately my life will decline and that one day I will die. I have seen addicts die. Even though I would talk and explain and try to nurture, I could not make an intervention for them successful.

I know how to manoeuvre addiction, just a little bit. I can.

I learned that addiction, enabling and codependency are things that can be canned. We can also open these cans whenever we choose to, or close them. Responsibility is just another can we can open. By opening the can of responsibility, we can break the cycle of addiction. We can also open the can of love, joy, grace and forgiveness, creating positive and healthy environments.

Ultimately, the quality of our lives depends on our ability to recognise and use the power of choice.

I can take hold of addiction and dance with it, and sometimes with my sway avoid a shipwreck. And in the darkest nights I can dance with addiction until daybreak, by showing the steps and my perception of the view from the times in my sway, but I need to have receptive partners to get them over to Lily at the Light Bridge.

Lily Bright is my superhuman force.

I am now the initiate, the master of competing ordeals, mistress of times, the delegated messenger, and such are my qualifications and curriculum vitae for being Luke's mom and wife to Zach, and mom to Alisa, all of whom I love with all of my heart, and if I could make their lives better, I'd be willing to do so.

And so, we are no longer in the same movie.

Things did change for the better. We nailed addiction into a coffin and made a tomb around the coffin. With our building blocks, we crafted masonry for this tomb.

This tomb is a sign in place of the superhuman force of addiction. The tomb holds our secret books as our prescription and our cure.

My inner ally, Lily Bright, helped me see what I knew deep down but missed in the chaos.

Sometimes Lily and I visit together. We sweep the tomb, Lily with freshly cut branches, and we chat about times and our lives.

Sometimes Lily sings.

And sometimes Lily dances.

www.ingramcontent.com/pod-product-compliance
Lightning Source LLC
LaVergne TN
LVHW020647100826
845148LV00012B/2355

* 9 7 8 0 7 9 6 1 1 1 9 1 3 *